Contents

Acknowledgements

The authors wish to thank Janet Stiling, Hilary Tolley, Seán Goddard and, above all, Judith Saywell, for skilled and forbearing assistance in the production of this volume. The Editor is grateful for an eagle eye cast by Michael Duffy over the proofs, to his colleagues on the Editorial Committee for their tactful encouragement and to the Publications Committee of the University for interest and support extending beyond the financial.

Introduction : the Interregnum

IVAN ROOTS

'If in time, as in place, there were degrees of high and low, I verily believe that the highest of time would be that which passed between the years 1640 and 1660.'[1] These are the opening words of Behemoth, Thomas Hobbes's 'history' of the Long Parliament, written but not published in 1668, when he was eighty, though apart from Parkinson's disease, still very much hale in mind and body. His remark is sometimes taken to signify a sort of approval of what happened in those two head-long decades. Nothing could be further from the truth. He goes on - and there is no doubt that in the dialogue of which it forms a part Thomas is talking to Hobbes -

> For he that thence, as from the Devil's Mountain,
> should have looked upon the world and observed
> the actions of men, especially in England, might
> have had a prospect of all kinds of injustice,
> and of all kinds of folly, that the world could
> afford....[2]

Other men who had felt their world wobble on its axis might well look back less in anger than with nostalgia, but for this political philosopher the only virtue of the upheaval was that the happenings had vindicated his doctrine of sovereignty. (He does not reflect that perhaps without the civil wars and their aftermath he might not have clinched his masterpiece, Leviathan).[3] For him pity it was that the wickedness and foolishness of those who, notably in the Long Parliament but much elsewhere, had dabbled in social, religious and political sedition, should have worked to the discomfort and worse of so many simple, less powerful, more amenable men. Even so, the notion of 'the highest time' is worth pursuing in the historian's quest for the true inwardness of these years. Whatever that may have been, the events themselves sprawled monstrously across the middle of the seventeenth century, decades which could never be forgotten, desirable though it might be for many to minimise them. Like America, another brave new world, the Interregnum, Restoration or no, could never be undiscovered again. In crisis once more in 1688-9, men remembered 'the late troubles',[4] for encouragement or more often, and in the end more decisively, for warnings.

The catastrophe of 1640-60 had causes. Historians, always hot for origins, have ever since Clarendon and Hobbes spent a great deal of time and ingenuity on causes. Some find them, as James Harrington did in the 1650s,[5] going at least as far back as the early Tudors; others, like Professor G.R. Elton and some of the quickly-established early-Stuart revisionist school, seem to find all the combustible material only in the few months preceding the outbreak of civil war in 1642.[6] (But was the Civil War the Revolution itself?) We should not be surprised to learn some day that there was not a civil war at all.

Reductionist and a rash of other interpretations have contributed to our understanding – 'King Charles and the conspirators', the Puritan Revolution, a bourgeois revolution, a conservative reaction against would-be absolutism or mere incompetence, Court versus Country, a general crisis, decentralisation v. centralisation, witch-hunters v. sceptics, alienated intellectuals, improving landlords, rising, falling, see-sawing gentry, a declining aristocracy, Providence, 'fate, chance, kings and desperate men', besides deep-seated (they are always deep-seated) social and economic forces – all these have been identified and called in to explain or explain away what happened.[7] All are in one way or another inadequate, are errors, indeed, but some have been fertile of truth and present-day historians, even aficionados of 'the new history' set off by the social sciences, can, while remaining genuinely puzzled, draw upon all or any of them to come up with hypotheses that may yet fuse into a fully explanatory compound. Even so, we should heed the reminder of Professor Lawrence Stone – he was referring to 'Court v. Country' but it applies to any other 'portmanteau' hypothesis – that by if adopting all or any of them

> it is possible powerfully to illuminate many things which were hitherto obscure, [we can do that] only at the expense of obscuring many others.[8]

But the historical enquiry should not stop short at causes. The course and consequences of the Interregnum now have a greater appeal. This change of emphasis has encouraged Drs Stephen Roberts and Derek Massarella, contributors to this volume, in their research to look, more closely than they might have done twenty years ago, at the 1650s, no longer a neglected decade to be rushed through to usher in the inevitable – if you approve – or sadly unavoidable – if you do not – Restoration of Charles II. There was more to the 1650s than that, as G.E. Aylmer's The State's Servants, Christopher Hill's God's Englishman and Milton and the English Revolution, T.D. Barnard's Cromwellian Ireland, F.D. Dow's Cromwellian Scotland and many of the essays in Aylmer's The Interregnum and the Christopher Hill festschrift show.[9] The interest in 'course' now extends beyond 1660 and the assumption that the Restoration somehow broke the back of the century or that it was a watershed, crossroads, turning-point, full-stop, fresh start or whatever comes under review. The theme is not only change but continuity, too, and both must be followed through into the 1660s, 1670s and beyond. It must not be forgotten that if some of the men of 1641 were men of '29, '21 or even '01, many of the men of '79 and '89 were men of '41, '49 and '59. All of these dates have some significance.

Some Intellectual Consequences, Christopher Hill's most recent book,[10] continuing his services to the historical profession, takes up briefly but with a wider range than ever before the problem of the results of what he persists in calling 'the English Revolution' disturbing the earth's diurnal course. It is a firework display – of rockets and damp squibs alike. Can all this, one wonders, be the results of a single revolution, let alone a mere interregnum? Probably not, but all that is offered (pace impatient reviewers) is worth some thought. Always be careful with fireworks – damp squibs can go off in your face. Another recent book, less pyrotechnic, The Stuart Age by Barry Coward,[11] surveying 1603-1714, may be commended for seeing the

century whole, refusing to pause for long at 1660 or even 1689, going so
far as to suggest that the Middle Ages came to an end in Robert Walpole,
with George I or George II, not Henry VII or Henry VIII, as the last
medieval, first modern king.

All this may well demote the Interregnum, to bring us down
from Hobbes's 'highest of time'. But it has not yet done so. Instead
it argues for continuing investigation of the 1640s and 1650s, both
within themselves and in a long perspective which can take in, for
instance, Conrad Russell's and others' new views of early Stuart
parliaments, not all of which see eye to eye, and the reconsiderations
in process of the restored monarchy, and of the glorious, the financial,
the commercial revolutions of the late seventeenth and early eighteenth
centuries. This present volume may seem not to contribute much to that
second search but its authors are aware of the need and do, they
believe, offer a few suggestions that might be pursued in a later volume
of the 'Exeter Studies in History'. The problems and possibilities of
local government, like many of its personnel, overlapped 1660 and went
on, both changed and continuous. The army that stood unshiftable and
like some watchful estate in the realm throughout the 1650s was at last
and with astonishing speed got rid of, most of it, though not all, at
the Restoration, but there was always a military dimension, however
fluctuating, to government and society from then on. In the last
decades of the seventeenth century no longer was there a union, formal
or otherwise, of England, Ireland and Scotland, but the history of the
peoples of 'these nations', as Cromwell addressed them, had been more
inextricably bound together than ever before by the events and
tendencies of the Interregnum. Constitutional arrangements since,
reflecting or, more characteristically, distorting political, social,
economic and cultural relations, weak or strong, have continued to
teeter, but if there were any genuine long-term consequences of the
Great Rebellion or of the Revolution the ways in which the constituents
of the British Isles have seen themselves and each other are surely a
necessary part of them. The moulds made then have been broken and thrown
away but something of the shape into which Oliver - and other men from
all three countries - crammed them can still be discerned.

Notes

1. T. Hobbes, Behemoth, or The Long Parliament, ed., F. Tonnies, 2nd
   edn., Introduction by M.M. Goldsmith (1969), p. 1.

2. Ibid., p. 1.

3. Whatever else it was, Leviathan (1651) was a contribution to the
   arguments over the Engagement under the Commonwealth. See
   Q. Skinner, 'Conquest and Consent: Thomas Hobbes and the Engagement
   Controversy' in G.E. Aylmer (ed.), The Interregnum (1972), pp. 79-
   98.

4. See, for example, the debates in the Convention Parliament of 1689,
   in which survivors of the Interregnum like John Birch and Sir John
   Maynard drew upon their long memories, W. Cobbett (ed.),
   Parliamentary History of England (36 vols., 1806-20), vol. v.

4

5. J. Harrington, Oceana (1656). Best edition in J.G.A. Pocock (ed.), The Political Works of James Harrington (Cambridge, 1977), pp. 155-359. See also R.G. A Copy of a Letter from an Officer of the Army in Ireland (1656; reprint, Exeter, 1974).

6. G.R. Elton, Studies in Tudor and Stuart Politics and Government (2 vols., Cambridge, 1974); C. Russell, 'Parliamentary History in Perspective 1604-1629', History, lxi (1976), pp. 1-27; C. Russell, Parliaments and English Politics 1621-1629 (Oxford, 1979); K. Sharpe (ed.), Faction and Parliament (Oxford, 1978).

7. The bibliography of this only selective list of interpretations is too vast to set out here. A useful starting point is R.C. Richardson, The Debate on the English Revolution (1976).

8. L. Stone, The Past and the Present (1981), p. 188.

9. D.H. Pennington and K. Thomas (eds.), Puritans and Revolutionaries: Essays in Seventeenth-Century History presented to Christopher Hill (Oxford, 1978).

10. C. Hill, Some Intellectual Consequences of the English Revolution (1980).

11. B. Coward, The Stuart Age (1981).

1. Union and Disunion in the British Isles 1637-1660

IVAN ROOTS

1. Approaches to the Interregnum

The events of the mid-seventeenth century may be approached in many ways. The usual measure is an English yard laid alongside developments in English national institutions or groups – the monarchy, the church, parliament, the privy council, the law courts, the peerage, the gentry. Everything comes to a focus in London – Westminster or Whitehall – thence radiating outwards. Another measure much used in the last two or three decades attempts a local dimension, particularly of county communities, each disturbed by internal as well as external tensions. So we find not only the civil war in Staffordshire but the civil war of Staffordshire, an intense struggle that might well be more absorbing there than the larger conflict. Doubt has recently been cast on the notion of a county community,[1] but quite apart from that historians have noted a role for other topographical units – regions (the far north, the forests), hundreds, cities, even villages – and for other sorts of communities, or particular interests such as trading companies, sects, professions.[2] A man making up his heart and mind to become, say, a royalist, might draw upon his membership of or association with a whole congeries of communities – topographical, professional, kinship, religious. The interactions, contradictions and ambivalences in an individual's or a group's assessment of where their own interests lay helps to explain why in the civil wars the pro-tagonists made shifting coalitions, hot for certainties but prone to get dusty answers. While some historians have scrabbled among the grass roots, others have taken a broader view, relating developments in England to others in Europe. Here is the notion of a general crisis made up of the Frondes, the revolts of the Catalans and of Portugal and so on, in which what was common – or can be made to seem so – was as important, if not more so, than what was peculiar to each of these strikingly contemporaneous conflagrations.[3] The nature of these and of the crisis of which they were apparently symptons are matters of continuing – though lately rather weakening – dispute, which has certainly shed some light, as well as dissipating a great deal of heat.

Somewhere among the grass roots, the national and the general European approaches there may be another avenue worth pursuing. Andrew Marvell's An Horation Ode on Cromwell's Return from Ireland tells us how 'by industrious valour' Oliver Cromwell managed 'to ruin the great work of time' and to 'cast the kingdoms old Into another mould'.[4] What is suggested here is that whatever else happened in the 1640s and 1650s there were striking changes in the relationships of the major con-stituents of the British Isles: England (with Wales), Scotland and Ireland. What we are looking at is in fact, not the English Revolution, the English Civil Wars, the late troubles in England, but a series of

interlocking perturbations amounting to a British Revolution - if,
indeed, there was a revolution. If we think of 'troubles' to the point
of violence it is clear at once that they did not begin in England. Not
until the spring of 1642 did some of the English start with great
reluctance seriously to contemplate taking up arms against one another
and it was late summer before the first shots were fired in anger.
Already by then Scots covenanters and Irish catholics were up in
rebellions (1638 and 1641 respectively) which were in themselves major
influences in bringing the English into civil war. It is, indeed,
impossible to understand the 1640s and 1650s without taking into account
not only God's Englishmen but also his Scots, Irish and Welshmen, too.
This means looking into each constituent in its own right but also from
each to its relations not merely with England but with the others. It
was a long period of slow, slow, quick, quick, slow changes throughout
the whole British Isles, few isolated, most in some way, not always
obvious but usually essentially, connected with each other. The notion
of a general crisis of the British Isles might seem more realistic
perhaps than one of Europe.

Themes for this crisis include unity and disunity, each of
which is relevant to complex situations, full of shifts and ambiguities.
The various 'nations' - as Cromwell called them in speeches during
which, characteristically, he also lumped them all, Welsh, Scots and
Irish together as English - were in many matters drawn together even as
in others they were drifting, even pulling, apart. Something that could
keep them together was geography. John of Gaunt's moat, the sea, was
defensive not merely to England but Magna Britannia and Hibernia too.[5]
The narrowest distance between these two islands, from Fairhead in
Antrim to the Mull of Kintyre, is only twelve miles, rather less than
the short Channel crossing from Dover to Calais. Between Scotland and
England and, of course, between England and Wales, there were only land
frontiers, hard to defend, easily and often crossed. The effects of the
geographical disposition of the kingdoms were diverse. On the one hand
it made for closeness of contacts, much coming and going, trade,
migration, cultural and linguistic exchange. On the other it encouraged
friction, competition, misunderstandings, border-raids, even invasion
with hopes of conquest. Sometimes it is easier to appreciate people
distant, rarely seen, than those nearer, on the spot as it were. The
quarrels of political neighbours are like domestic squabbles, often
fierce, even murderous, though ironically, soonest patched up - until
next time, anyway. What can be felt in the mid-seventeenth century -
and can be still glimpsed today, when relationships within these islands
are again in flux - is a mingled urge towards independence and
interdependence, and a sense of common interest shading into hostility.

2. Scotland before the Covenant

First Scotland. Bishop Burnet's remark that 'the late Civil
Wars' had their 'first beginning' there is often quoted, but not always
in full. He goes on:

> there can be no clear understanding of what
> followed until these first disorders there be
> truly stated.[6]

The historian, then, even the one with an exclusively English concern, must keep at least half an eye upon Scotland. Whatever happened in England was preceded by and went along - not always in parallel, nor in the same plane, nor even at the same pace - with developments in Scotland. The two kingdoms were already in 1637 ravelled up together. The Scottish National Covenant was certainly an expression of a distinct Scottish nationalism - a call for breaking a real or imaginary dependence upon England and thus in some sort anti-English, proclaiming a refusal to be dragged along on the coat-tails of a richer, more populous neighbour with social, cultural, economic traits and interests different from, even somewhat inimical to, the Scots'. But that is not the only story that can or should be made of the Covenant. Look back to the mid-sixteenth century. The English Reformation had been mostly led by the Tudor Crown - the Scottish one, which had come later, was driven against the Stuarts' indignation. The English, a stiff-necked confident people, stressed their long traditions of being an elect nation - to the point of claiming that God is English.[7] The Scots' religious experience was different. John Knox and his associates felt they could appeal only to a more recent intervention by God and so elucidated the immediate intentions of Providence in a specific gesture, one making Scotland a covenanted nation. But they thought that the ultimate impact must surely be the same both sides of the border. God expected both his old English and his new Scots to embrace one true religion and to establish that by a common effort, a British effort. God then, was British, or would be if men would let him. Speaking English and encouraging that tongue in Scotland, Knox and company saw themselves not as strangers to England

> but in a manner your own countrymen, so the Isle
> [i.e. Great Britain] is a common country to us
> both....one of the same religion.

Some were optimistic enough to extend that aspiration to Ireland: imagining 'a reformed Ireland....brought to a perfection of obedience....'. The British Isles would then have become a 'certain monarchy in itself and in the ocean divided from the rest of the world'. (The sea again, seen as a barrier externally, but also an internal binding force.)[8]

So a Scottish national consciousness, inextricably associated with the Kirk - than which there could be nothing on earth more valuable - argued for a more, not a less, intimate relationship - even a 'brotherhood' - with England. Similar church discipline and doctrine in England would guarantee their survival in Scotland. Supporters in the National Covenant went so far as to refer to

> the greatest blessing that God has bestowed on
> this isle....next the Christian faith was the
> union of the two kingdoms under one head,

that of James VI and I.[9] It was a sentiment not much shared in England. James told the English that they had gained from union with Wales - 'and is not Scotland greater than Wales?'. That, of course, was the rub. Wales was too small to threaten any aspect of English life. Scotland had a larger population, a greedy untamed nobility, a long tradition of anti-English alliance with foreign powers. A firmer union seemed a threat and James's identification of himself in 1604 as 'the husband and the whole isle is my lawful wife' was unappealing.[10] James himself went on to concentrate his attention on England, governing Scotland by proxy with his pen.[11] Under his successor, the Stuart monarchy became even more remote from its origins. Sharing the common-sense drive of European rulers with diversified territories to bring them into some kind of uniformity, Charles I, though, in fact, he did not hand Scotland over to his English privy council, ruled from London, robbing his northern kingdom of the presence of a royal court, the rewards of patronage and whatever, reminding Scots of Henry VII's pre-diction of the likely fruits of the marriage of his daughter Margaret to James IV - a union that was 'an accession not of England to Scotland, but of Scotland to England'.[12] The distrust already aroused by James VI's Articles of Perth was increased by his son's own Act of Revocation and the assignment to the bishops of a direct, indeed, a conspicuous role in secular as well as in spiritual affairs. His behaviour during his visit in 1633 for his coronation, the ritual then, the consequent canons of uniformity and finally the new prayer book raised the cry of 'the Kirk in danger!'. The upshot was the Covenant of 1638, which looked as if it were both anti-monarchical and anti-English and was not.[13]

3. Scotland from the Covenant to the Engagement

        The Covenant was, in fact, directed against the king's evil counsellors, who were more Scots than English, and against religious innovations - chiefly associated with William Laud - which were known to be unacceptable also to many in England. Covenanters were aware, too, of political and social strains and disappointments in England not unlike their own. For example, Laud's stepping up of tithes paralleled the Revocation. Immediate contacts with English puritans hinted at a possible common cause of religion,[14] liberties, laws and estates. The chauvinism of the Covenant did not preclude a recognition that if Charles I of Scotland was being misled, so was Charles I of England. Hence some Scots were not displeased that their 'business' brought on, first, the Short, and then the Long Parliament, since it was certain that the king would not be incontinently provided by them with the wherewithall to bring the rebels to heel. The presence of a Scottish army in the north of England and the treaty of Ripon ensured that for his part Charles could not easily dispense with a parliament bent on redress of grievances which included the elimination of Laud and Strafford, men as unfit for the state of Scotland as for that of England. Charles's clear recognition of links between his critics in both kingdoms was underlined by his northern journey in the summer of 1641 when he set out to separate them by offering concessions in Scotland. The Additional Instruction was John Pym's answer to the king's patent tactics there,[15] and in the event all Charles succeeded in doing was to heighten the political temperature within each kingdom rather than to incite animosities between them.

        Then came the Ulster rebellion of October 1641, which directly affected Scots as well as English interests, and brought the core of opposition in each country, if anything, even tighter together. Once civil war broke out in England, Pym exploited the situation by working for a Solemn League and Covenant between the two countries.

Attained before he died in 1643, this was one of his many contributions
to parliament's ultimate victory, though not as major as it was first
thought it would be. What the English wanted was a civil league and the
Scottish army that would go with it. For the Scots it was the Covenant
that appealed most, making explicit what was implied in 1638 that both
nations must work together in the sight of God to preserve the Kirk by
extending the one reformed and true religion into England. Hence the
bitterness of that inflexible Covenanter Robert Baillie about the
failure of the Assembly of Divines at Westminster to come up with
anything more than 'a lame Erastian presbytery'. That was not just an
immediate blow at Scotland but a betrayal of traditional hopes of a
dedicated British nation of Scots and English confidently striding
together, elect and covenanted, 'bosom brethren, one flesh and
blood'[16]. Some Covenanters had even talked of taking an elated
British army into the Continent to spread the really reformed religion
there, while in Ireland another jointly would reduce the rebels,
spreading presbyterianism, praising God and at the same time securing
Scotland and England.

The Scots, in fact, wanted religious unity to the point of
obsession, pursuing 'one union of this island, one form of Kirks, one
confession of faith, one catechism, one directory for the worship of
God'.[17] That spiritual aim, they recognised, called for civil union,
too. So they accepted a Committee of Both Kingdoms. So did the English
parliament, but its motivation was only secondarily religious. The
Scottish army seemed essential in the dark days when it was first called
in. Certainly its presence in the north of England tied down royalist
forces there, but as the English parliamentary armies gradually advanced
towards superiority, there were reports that some 'did leap for joy' at
Scottish failures. Even presbyterians were inclined to see union as an
invitation to Scots, who though presbyterian were still Scots, to
interfere in English affairs, giving them an 'unwelcome power over us'.
The growth of Independency and the proliferation of sects meant even
more resentment of Scottish rigidity while intensifying strains between
army and parliament which would eventually become political. Similarly
in Scotland itself Montrose's victories, won in part with Irish catholic
forces, made Scottish domestic politics more complicated.[18] So
between 1646 and 1649 both kingdoms were in continuous tension, if not
revolution, even if, as English revisionist historians are rushing to
point out, there was also consensus on many points of parliamentary
politics.

Charles's surrender to the Scots reflected his considered
judgment that it would not be hard to break up the uneasy political
alliances forged by his enemies – and so he would be king again. For
the Scots to transfer him to Parliament was an unwelcome surprise,
suggesting that there were still optimists about who could envisage an
ultimate union. But the cynical Engagement he negotiated in 1647
shattered residual unity again between the Scots and the English,
between the English army and the parliament and in Scotland among the
Covenanters themselves. The second Civil War testifies to Charles's
success in finding means towards his objective, his execution to his
failure to reach it.

4. Scotland in the 1650s and beyond

The Scots were now a fragmented nation undergoing political and even social revolution.[19] Though no party was willing to accept the unilateral English abolition of the national monarchy, not everyone was convinced of sincerity in the readiness of Charles, Prince of Wales, to take the Covenant. It was apparent that he came to Scotland on his way to England and though he promised 'to endeavour a complete union of the kingdoms', each of which had 'an unquestionable and undeniable interest in his person as king of both',[20] many felt that once in London he would follow James VI and Charles I as an absentee. Defeats by Cromwell at Dunbar (1650) and Worcester (1651) were not unwelcome to every patriotic Scot. (Equally if Charles had won many an English royalist would have been unhappy that he should receive his southern kingdom back from alien hands). As it happened, Cromwell's victories would lead on to a union, but one in a new mould, into which Scotland was poured by an iron hand in an iron glove. There was no question now of the Kirk being imposed upon England, indeed, its very existence in Scotland was in jeopardy, given a state religious policy which offered toleration while preventing presbyterians from patently political preaching. Scotland over the next few years was ruled in English interests 'as when the poor bird is embodied into the hawk that has eaten it up'.[21] Yet things could have been worse. There was no attempt to make Scotland a colony, thrown open to planters and adventurers, though the Rump set up a Committee (September 1651) to draft a measure declaring 'the right of this Commonwealth to so much of Scotland as is now under [our] forces'. This resulted in a bill 'asserting the right of England to Scotland'. But that brutal claim soon gave way to a more feasible scheme to create 'one commonwealth and free state' out of the two nations.[22] Following discussions with appropriate (i.e. reasonably amenable) Scottish interest groups, 'deputies' came down to London. Worried that the union intended was undefined and carried with it their acceptance of 'we know not what', they were still talking it over when Cromwell expelled the Rump. Barebone's, too, considered union but resigned before anything was settled.

The Instrument of Government assumed a union with Scottish (and Irish) representation in an imperial parliament. Ordinances issued in 1654 under clause xxx of the Instrument provided for a union with Scotland at least and for distribution of parliamentary seats in both countries.[23] But neither contained anything like a Solemn League and Covenant or a Committee of Both Kingdoms. Scotland remained under a military-dominated Council of State and was administratively in essence a subordinate entity, though given a prospect of 'healing and settling' into a more relaxed relationship. However, the first Protectorate parliament failed to confirm the union and other relevant ordinances. The second parliament accepted the union in the measure of 12 April 1657 which confirmed a mass of ordinances 'in a lump'. So did the Humble Petition and Advice, which had the considerable advantage - or so it was expected - over the Instrument of having a parliamentary sanction.[24] But in the 1659 parliament (Richard Cromwell's) commonwealthsmen, still smarting from the expulsion of 1653, the abrupt dissolution of February 1658, and frustrated by their inability in spite of their mastery of procedure to prevent formal recognition of 'the Single Person', insisted on assailing to the point of 'great noise and horrid confusion' the presence in their midst of 'Scottish members' who were seen both as

elements alien in culture and interests and in the pockets of the
exective - which some, though perhaps not all, of them certainly were.
Burton's Diary records a great deal of what was said and it testifies to
the stubborn survival of traditional Scotophobia, reinforced by more
recent experience, resistant to the argument of 'the Court' that union
between England, Ireland and Scotland would become 'a strong treble cord
twisted together' that would not be easily broken, unless foolishly it
were untwisted. Scotland was sneered at as a province 'at best', its
inhabitants 'foreigners' with no colour to be represented at
Westminster. If Scots were admitted why not members from Jamaica? On
the other hand there were some vigorous defences of union, calling on
the long and short-term interests of both Scotland and England. But the
main thrust of the debates was towards criticism of the character and
very existence of the Protectorate and they are another illustration - a
particularly vivid and circumstantial one - of the way in which the
interlocking of the three kingdoms had an impact upon the internal
politics of each.[25]

Throughout the Protectorate many Englishmen thought they had
been particularly generous to the Scots in imposing union. 'What
greater favour could they cast upon you?'. In his Memoirs Edmund Ludlow
looked back to 'how great a condescension' it was.[26] For many Scots
it was an insult and an injury. The Kirk, denied its General Assembly,
saw it as even worse than an obscene travesty of the British union they
had envisaged only a decade before. Favouring diversity and controversy
in religion, the Cromwellian union spat in the face of a rigid
presbyterianism that still could not think it possible it might be
mistaken. But some Scots, more venal or maybe more politic, could
glimpse the two countries 'homogeneated by naturalisation and the mutual
enjoyment of the same privileges and immunities', even sharing the same
burdens. This would produce a real 'Great Britain'. Meanwhile
resistance continued in the craggy and papist Highlands where the
English, unenthusiastic even about the more settled Lowlands, deplored a
wild people who 'generally speak Irish (sic), go only with plads about
their middle, both men and women', 'savage beasts', 'bloody-minded',
'base and beggarly', living - wilfully seems to be implied - in houses
'only of earth and turfs'.[27] Union with people like that could hardly
be contemplated.

When the Rump was restored in May 1659 it repudiated
naturally enough - though perhaps impolitically - all that had been done
in its 'exile'. But, significantly on a Scottish initiative, a bill for
union was brought in, to be nipped in the bud at the expulsion in
August. It is ironical that when the Restoration of 1660 came to
England it came in effect from Scotland. George Monck's success in
settling North Britain,[28] ostensibly in the name and interests of the
various régimes he had served under in the 1650s, enabled him to march
his brain-washed army slowly upon London during the winter of 1659-60,
confident that behind him there was an urge for order and stability
among Scots, many of whom pressed him to see the union maintained. The
Rump, restored yet again, toyed with the notion of an act of union but
dissolved itself before it neared completion. The Convention of 1660
did nothing about it and Charles II came back without any commitment to
it - or for that matter to the Covenant he had sworn to ten years
before. So a separate Scotland, quite unrepresented in either chamber
at Westminster, got back its own parliament and its own administration.
But both were under heavy pressure from English court-politicians and

the country was greatly discriminated against economically and socially. The reign of Charles II was a black period which made the 1650s seem like a golden age. For his own reasons Charles II was not inimical to negotiations for a union in 1668-69. Scottish commissioners once again made the long trek to London. Discussions echoed the phraseology of the past: 'two kingdoms....united into one monarchy....inseparably and... the name of that monarchy shall be Great Britain'.[29] The scheme foundered largely because of Scottish disappointment at the small amount of representation adjudged sufficient for them and because of English coolness to the whole 'package'. When the Revolution of 1688-89 raised the spectre of a separate Scottish monarchy in the old Stuart line, a few concessions were given to them by the new one under William III. But it was not until the Hanoverian succession was in clear prospect under Anne, that the matter was seriously canvassed again 'as necessary not for any actual good it could possibly do but to avoid a probable evil'.[30] The crisis was resolved by a union painfully formed in 1707, one in which Scotland lost her parliament, but retained some of her national institutions like the Kirk and the legal system. It seemed to be - was certainly so put over - in the interests of significant groups in both countries. Though it was assailed fiercely from the start it has somehow survived to come under heavy fire in recent years when relationships within the British Isles seem to skirt again the brink of crisis, with many Scots preferring 'a poor independent sovereignty' for Scotland to 'a small share in a great one'.[31]

5. Ireland before the Ulster Rebellion

If seventeenth-century English attitudes towards the Scots were born of ignorance strengthened by prejudice, so, too, were those they adopted towards the Irish - and they were even more intolerant. Politically England and Ireland had had contacts older and more intimate than those between independent Scotland and England. The connexion went back to the reign of Henry II in the twelfth century when barons like Richard Strongbow, Earl of Pembroke, realised the possibilities of carving out territories and the political power that went with them over there. The aim became one of reducing the bulk of the native Irish to helots. Wave after wave of immigrants, not large in number maybe but vigorous and greedy, imposed a range of would-be élites who became collectively under the label 'the Old English' neo-Irish. By conquest and confiscation they acquired the land before they became the land's. But gradually they did develop interests and ways of life which were not those of the motherland, where the attention of the government was all too often distracted from Ireland by internal problems, like the Wars of the Roses, or by policies pursued elsewhere - notably towards France and Scotland. But the English crown never completely gave up a direct concern for what went on in Dublin and beyond. Ireland was well on the way to being an English colony long before Elizabethan expeditions were sent to North America. The expanding and contracting Pale around Dublin, where only, for centuries, English power was really effective and outside which its authority hardly existed, paralleled the narrow American seaboard beyond which was Indian country. But as in America the foothold was bound sooner or later to turn into a platform for the taking of the whole country. Irish aspirations for independence with or without allegiance to the English crown were always dashed by the fact that England could and did cut their island off from direct continental contacts, especially out of fear that otherwise Ireland might become a base for invasion - as it was for the Pretenders in the reign of Henry VII, who as an invader himself could appreciate the problem. It assumed great importance with the Reformation. Both the native Irish and the Old English clung to catholicism, each group in its own way associating religion with an incipient nationalism and making it a potent symbol of 'Ireland their own'. In turn Irish popery increased English distrust and encouraged a will to break out of the Pale until the whole island was under control - and paying for it. Ironically the first systematic moves towards plantation - settled colonisation - came under the catholic rule of Philip and Mary. Queen's and King's counties suggested a pattern of dispossession and seizure that would endure for a century or more. By the middle of the reign of Elizabeth I conquest was the consistent policy and English settlers and the armies that preserved them took increasingly the line that the native Irish in their bogs were

> little better than cannibals that do hunt one
> another, more uncivil, more unreliant, more
> barbarous and more brutish in their customs and
> demeanours than in any part of the world [32]

and that it was therefore 'a civic duty' for 'duty and obedience' to be imposed on them 'by fear and force'. Those whom we intend to exploit we must first make contemptible.

Revolts followed by confiscations and implantations into the seventeenth century determined that relationships with the various strains of the Irish population would remain tense. The union of the crowns of England and Scotland in 1603 was an event equally in Irish history. Scots had, of course, been interested in Ireland over a long period. Common Celtic origins, linguistic and cultural affinities lasting well into the later Middle Ages, and geography - Scotland, remember, is closer to Ireland than either England or Wales is - all these argued for impacts upon on another. Under the Bruces conquest itself was attempted as something more than a mere counter to English aspirations there. Thenceforth concern, though fluctuating, never petered out. Under Elizabeth I Scottish penetration of nearby Ulster began and was not resisted by her. The aftermath of the Flight of the Earls in 1607 quickened the process. Not unexpectedly the Scots, whether on royal plantations, as individual adventurers or simply as hopeful tenants on the estates of (often absentee) English landlords, proved to be dour, determined settlers.[33] The character of the province of Ulster was largely fixed by them. It survives to this day - the Rev. Ian Paisley refers to himself as an Ulster Scot. The religious complexion of Ireland now included presbyterianism, lay and clerical, for the Scots took ministers with them. This ran up against the 'Anglican' policy for Church of Ireland pursued by Lord Deputy Thomas Wentworth, inspired by Laud. When Scotland rose in 1638 Wentworth was quick, too quick in fact, to sense a likely collusion between Ulster Scots and Covenanters and to see them using the province as 'a back door' into England. He resisted Hamilton's scheme to colonise Derry where the City of London was dawdling, even though like himself Hamilton was a king's man. He sought to impose 'a black oath' whereby Scots in Ireland were formally to express repudiation of the Covenant. Yet Ulster was not socially, politically nor even religiously, a mirror-image of noble-dominated Kirk-ridden Lowland Scotland and Wentworth clumsily excited avoidable animosities.[34] More to his point would have been an alliance of Ulster Scots with the newer Protestant English

settlers in the implementation of his aim of converting fragmented
Ireland into a single polity contributing to the interests of the Anglo-
Scottish monarchy with which he identified his own. It meant creating
an Ireland as uniform as he wanted England itself to become. Instead he
made himself more and more isolated and when he was called back home to
cope, too late, with 'the Scottish business' his system such as it was
collapsed.

6. Ireland during the 1640s

      The Long Parliament met under the shadow of a possible coup
from Strafford (as he now was) based on the intervention of a
disciplined, largely papist Irish army. 'You have an army in Ireland
you may use to reduce this kingdom' - he could have meant England or
Scotland or both. Certainly both Covenanters and the English
parliamentary majority looked askance at Ireland, with the former
anxious to keep their forces on foot in all three kingdoms and the
latter to get rid of Strafford, to keep an eye on the unreliable royal
army in the north of England and to prevent the king from coming to
terms with the Scots there. When rebellion was raised by the native
Irish - papists to a man - the Scots were quick to send forces there to
protect their own interests. Curiously enough though it was said the
Irish hated the Scots perfectly in the very early stages of the rising
they left them alone - no doubt in hopes of separating them from the
English.[35] If that was so, the gambit failed and soon English and
Scots were a single enemy. The rebellion, which dramatically intensi-
fied English domestic politics, was also formative in Scottish internal
affairs. By the end of 1641 the crisis was already one sucking in three
kingdoms at odds with each other and within themselves. It needed only
the outbreak of actual fighting in England to engulf the whole British
Isles.

      Very quickly the Old English were in alliance with the native
rebels, under a confederate banner proclaiming support for 'one God, one
King, one Country'. (The king was conveniently misled by evil advisers,
a misfortune kings have been in all ages prone to). Though Charles said
at once that suppression was 'his chief business' he was in fact very
dilatory about it, giving a priority to seeking political, soon to
become military, support for action at home. Pym and his associates
were unwilling to trust him with a military wherewithal that might be
turned inward upon themselves.[36] The Grand Remonstrance, with which
they consciously risked breaking the uneasy parliamentary front, raised
inter alia the whole question of military power in England - and perhaps
even as early - that of sovereignty, too - and led on to the Militia
Ordinance, the Commissions of Array, the Nineteen Propositions and the
King's Answer, paper skirmishes, postures of defence, and at length
military standards raised. Civil war, which was the least expected
outcome of the collapse of the Personal Government in 1640, had come by
August 1642 to England (and Wales), Scotland and Ireland. There were
armies everywhere, covenanted, confederated, associated and whatever.
The military - and it followed political - consequences of all this were
incalculable.

      Though both king and Parliament concentrated on developments
within England and Wales, they could never quite forget Ireland. Each
intended sooner or later to reduce and punish the insubordinate colony.

Charles, however, could see an immediate advantage towards his English objectives in coming to some arrangement with rebels who claimed, like Parliament, to fight actually on his behalf, to extricate him from evil advisers, Jesuits on the one interpretation, protestants on the other. An Irish truce would release for intervention in England and Wales his own forces presently bogged down over there and perhaps even allow the recruitment of some rebel troops into his armies. Charles might argue that since it was clearly in the interests of the parliamentarians 'to improve and continue the rebellion'[37], a negotiated break in the Irish struggle was not only necessary for his own preservation but for that of his loyal subjects in both kingdoms. Hence he entered without shame into 'the Cessation' of 1643. 'Politically disastrous' it certainly was, alienating Parliament further and dividing the royalists. It was hard to counter the propaganda charge that the king was inveterately 'soft' on popery. But initially at least it did give him some military gains, more, it has been suggested recently, than has been commonly supposed.[38] Troops from Ireland stiffened the royalist effort in North Wales and its borders – and Wales was, after all, a 'chief nursery' of his armies. This accretion of strength may well have made the war in England last longer, while in Scotland Montroses's spectacular advances could have owed something to Irish levies, distracting such attention as the Covenanters were able to give to their supporting role to Parliament in northern England. Since many Scots shared the English estimate of the 'cruel savagery' of the Irish, the Cessation inflamed opinion there, too.

The Cessation did not in fact mean complete and unbroken peace in Ireland. The Scots army in Ulster, supplied and encouraged from the Lowlands, fought on and as soon as Charles's defeat in England was certain it was politically desirable for Parliament to contemplate an early campaign throughout Ireland. The 'presbyterian' parliamentary majority regarded the new Model as 'a mere mercenary army' at their behest.[39] Why not send some of its regiments over there, where they would be decently distanced from English politics – consensus or otherwise – and kept busy about useful tasks assigned to them by their civilian masters? Who pays the piper calls the tune – but only so long as he pays up. Already by early 1647 army pay was in arrears, the soldiers' professional grievances were palpable and their redress could easily become a political aspiration. The regiments nominated refused to go and before long the army was an estate in the realm. Thus Ireland like Scotland remained a living issue in English political developments. 'The search for a settlement' which has been fairly taken to characterise the next few years was not just an English but an emphatically British requirement.

The execution of the king, formative as we have seen in both Scottish internal politics and Anglo-Scotch relations, marked a stage also for Ireland. The Rump was determined to break the Cessation, to crush the long festering rebellion there and to make the Irish pay financially and otherwise for the nuisance they had been now for nearly a decade. Moreover, security demanded denial of the island to royalists in exile and to their potential foreign allies, who now included those Scots who were hankering after their House of Stuart. Ireland once conquered, the confiscations intended since 1642 could be effected, with some at least of the proceeds diverted to reduce the English armies' dangerous arrears. So Cromwell was sent as the instrument of that

Providence in whom he trusted - though characteristically he extracted from the Rump cash enough to pay his troops for a brisk campaign, being as aware as Strafford had been that money is as much the sinews of military discipline as it is of civil government. Even so, his preparations coincided with the last real fling of regimental radicalism in mutinies at Northampton and Burford - somewhat reminiscent of the 1647 resistance to drafting to Ireland. As it was, the suppression of the army Levellers augured well for a swift effective campaign. The story of Cromwell in Ireland is well known. Of its military impact there is no doubt. The terror that was part of it and its significance in our estimate of Cromwell's character and achievement remain matters of living controversy. What can be said is that his actions were in line with some contemporary views of legitimate military tactics and were resonant with 'respectable' English attitudes towards the Irish. Marvell's Horation Ode with all its ambiguities about Cromwell and his English ambitions sees no occasion for a moral judgment upon this particular episode.[40]

7. Cromwellian Ireland

Within months most of Ireland was reduced. Though it was the Lord's work, Cromwell himself clearly regarded the campaign as a distraction from his ultimate ambitions, which lay elsewhere. He soon returned home leaving his adroit son-in-law, Henry Ireton, to complete the conquest. Ireton was dead within a couple of years - an event not without significance for England as well as Ireland - and it took several more years within a de facto union to effect anything like a settlement. Cromwell himself, even as Lord Protector of the three kingdoms, seemed only fitfully interested and if we are to speak of Cromwellian Ireland it is either in a very loose sense or with specific reference not so much to Oliver as to Henry Cromwell, who overlapping and then following the insipid George Fleetwood as Lord Deputy, moulded policy there from 1655-59. The effort could have been one merely of conquest, of unmitigated punishment and revenge - making 'a wilderness and calling it peace'. Many in England and Scotland would have approved of that. In fact what was done was of some complexity, with developments going in different directions at different paces, responding in part to political tergiversations back home and in part to the diverse attitudes of the administrators on the spot, chiefly military, some of them like Edmund Ludlow quite hostile to the very existence of the Protectorate.[41] In part, too, the process of change and continuity was affected by the actions and reactions of various Irish interest and pressure groups - from the natives (not much) to the new adventurers and the holders of debentures on confiscated land. (Many of these were rank-and-file soldiers who disposed of them for quick money to speculators, mostly their own officers - a power bloc which would in some measure survive the Restoration). Once again Scotland cannot be left out of the tally. Conflicts there between Resolutioners (ready to accept Charles II) and Remonstrants (inveterately inimical to him) spread to Ulster, presenting the administration with such political as well as religious problems that a transplantation of Resolutioners to the south-west was seriously contemplated. Eventually more conciliatory attitudes on both sides eased the situation. In this a prominent part was played by Roger Boyle, Lord Brogill, Lord President of the Scottish Council in the mid-1650s.[42]

Broghill, son of 'the great Earl of Cork', was a leading light among 'the Old Protestants' (the 'new' English – and Scots – of the Elizabethan and early Stuart plantations). The likely organiser of 'the kinglings' who in the parliament of 1656-58 offered Cromwell the crown, Broghill was a man of three kingdoms, whose policy within and between all three was to create stability by establishing what would be in effect a coalition of moderates and conservatives, drawing in 'the natural rulers' of the kingdoms. For Ireland his means was to get Henry Cromwell, whose sensible 'art-of-the-possible' temperament he quickly discerned, to work for the political ascendancy of the well-landed Old Protestants over the Catholics, whether natives or Old English on the one hand, and the new Protestants – adventurers or debenture-holders – on the other. In England Oliver Cromwell had to refuse the crown and much of Broghill's programme faltered. In Scotland ultimate authority still lay in the Commander-in-Chief, George Monck, more consistently enigmatic than encouraging. But from 1656 onwards Henry Cromwell did come somewhat more reliably up to expectations.

There was, we know, a land revolution in Ireland during the Interregnum. It has been estimated that in 1640 nearly two-thirds of Ireland was in catholic (chiefly Old English) hands but by 1660 little more than a fifth remained there.[43] Many of the new owners were, of course, debenture-holders and adventurers and one would have expected the political balance to have tipped towards them. In fact as the 1650s wore on it went to the Protestants previously settled – the Old Protestants, the Broghills as it were. They had to work for it. Many had been royalists in the 1640s, suspected of malignancy for years afterwards by propagandists of the Good Old Cause. Henry Cromwell, beginning to direct policy from 1655 onwards, was more willing to offer 'oblivion', recognising how much stability across the three states which somehow or other had come into the charge of his father – to whom he was devoted – depended upon the co-operation of men with a permanent stake – 'a fixed interest', in Ireton's term – in society. As early as 1649 some Old Protestants had shewn a willingness to give that co-operation sensing that since the military régime was clearly powerful enough to stay for at least a while, it would be impolitic, if not self-spiting, to offer blind opposition. If they had articulated their instinctive reactions they would no doubt have used some of the same arguments as those deployed at the same time in England in support of the Engagement of 1650. But their line generally was as practical as that of the Earl of Leicester in taking the Engagement – he wanted to be able to take tenants in arrears to court.[44] The Old Protestants set out to mitigate the policy of 'Hell or Connaught', not because of any squeamishness about the hardship it inflicted upon the natives, but because the exile of 'the meaner sort of people' would rob themselves of the cheap labour force they needed for the proper exploitation of their estates. Recruitment of protestant field-workers from England and Wales would have helped but was unlikely – settlement in Ireland was even less appealing to 'the inferior sort' than in America. But the Old Protestants had no objection to the transportation of catholic proprietors and the confiscation and redistribution of their estates – indeed there was little they could see against it. But many military men and some Commissioners wanted revenge for the legendary massacres of '41, blood calling out for blood; they would wipe out popery at all levels of society. That urge was strong among the Baptists and some of these were also vigorous opponents of the Protectorate on ideological grounds. Maintaining contacts with critics in England - as did common-wealthsmen, fifth monarchists and sectaries - they were prepared to be obstructive on both sides of the Irish Sea. The army in Ireland can indeed be considered a major centre of opposition to the sort of settlement with 'somewhat of monarchical in it' that Broghill was backing in England and Scotland. Nearer at home the Old Protestants saw in army debenture-holders, more and more of them officers, well-placed political and economic rivals. Unlike the new adventurers, often absentees, some leaving their lands to lie literally waste, debenture-holders were on the spot, many ready to stay and make the most of what they could get hold of. All this encouraged the Old Protestants to look to Henry Cromwell. Kept well-informed by John Thurloe of what was happening in England and Scotland, he was inclined to see them as a counter to the instability inherent in the régime with which he had to cope.

The Henrician settlement in Ireland was watched from and discussed in all three kingdoms. Apart from its general impact it had a particular influence at a critical time. Under the terms of the Humble Petition and Advice Oliver Cromwell could nominate his own successor as Protector. On his deathbed he appears to have given his voice to his eldest surviving son, Richard, inexperienced, untried. This decision made for comment at the time and has ever since. Why did he not choose Henry, able, tested, bright? One reason must have been that Henry by his very policies in Ireland had excited in the army in Ireland animosities which had spread to England. He was considered personally ambitious and too open to, if not party to, the manoeuvres of the ex-malignant (and some probably still royalist) Old Protestants and over-tolerant, too, to Catholics. His moves, somewhat successful, towards stability hinted at a reduction in the need for substantial military forces. The opposition to the sitting of Irish members, which was as fierce as that to the Scots in the debates in Richard's parliament [45] was perhaps as much against Henry as against the Protectorate itself. This view is reinforced by the speed with which the restored Rump put Henry out of office and set out to rule Ireland more or less direct from Westminister and on very different lines - with heavy taxes to relieve fiscal burdens in England and economic restrictions which would impinge on Old Protestant enterprise. The result was the de facto union of England and Ireland which was less acceptable now to the Old Protestants and from then on they worked against it. Broghill might have assured Thurloe in 1659 that they would never set up for themselves making Ireland 'a back door to let Charles Stuart into England....interest as well as duty will keep us from so ruinous a wickedness'.[46] 'Interest cannot lie' said Harrington at about the same time, but men can lie about it and it is likely that Broghill was a royalist well before George Monck revealed himself in the spring of 1660. An Irish con-vention dominated by Old Protestants met at the same time as the English one to add its weight to those summoning Charles II back but, as important, to do what it could to retain and extend the ascendancy they had worked so hard for throughout the 1650s. On the whole they succeeded.

Throughout the seventeenth century whether under early or later Stuarts or during the Interregnum Ireland was regarded in England as

> far enough [away] to be treated as a colonisable area, but near enough to be governable by the English state in its own interests rather than be abandoned to the colonists and theirs.[47]

The attitude of the colonists themselves, whether Old Protestants or the newcomers of the 1650s, was ambiguous. They wanted to be left alone, but at the same time they could recognise a need for the support, indeed the protection, of England against internal dissension even if that was not pushed to the point of open rebellion, with or without help from abroad. Memories of men of '41 survived in Ireland, even as they survived of different men of '41 in England. What the English protestant ascendancy, merging with the Scots of Ulster, did not want in 1660 and afterwards was a union, de facto or otherwise, that would restrict themselves. They had taken advantage of the Cromwellian régime and intended fully to take advantage of its successors. It is difficult and quite unnecessary to disagree with Dr. Toby Barnard's conclusion that the character of the Protestant ascendancy was 'largely formed' in the 1650s and was the Cromwellians' 'enduring contribution to Ireland'.[48] As such it was one of the few identifiable permanent consequences of the Interregnum – and it was one of significance not only for Ireland but for Scotland, England and Wales – indeed, the whole British Isles.

8. Conclusion: The General Crisis of the British Isles

If there is any value in seeking common features in or interactions between coincident events, it is more likely to be found in such intimately-related entities as England, Wales, Scotland and Ireland than in the disparate – still in spite of the EEC wildly disparate – elements of Western Europe. Englishmen were directly involved in Scotland and Ireland, Scots in England and Ireland, Irishmen (though admittedly in smaller numbers) in England and Scotland and Welshmen in all of them during the 1640s and 1650s. Few if any of these people were sucked into the Frondes, the Revolt of the Catalans or Cossack risings on the remote steppes of Central Asia. The close relations of the constituents of the British Isles were made by geography, long history and interest. The last of these binding forces was at its tightest perhaps in those excited years between the Covenant of 1637 and the surprising Restoration of 1660, during which some common institutions were set up, if only temporarily – the Committee of Both Kingdoms and those unwillingly imperial parliaments of the Protectorate. This was something more than the union of the crowns of England and Scotland in 1603 and the long-standing claims of the English crown to all of Ireland. The comings and goings between the islands and over the land-frontiers were more frequent than ever before and for a long time afterwards – and the movements were not solely those of men in arms, but of ideas, political, cultural and scientific, not touched upon here but certainly an instrinsic part of the new moulding, which was broken though perhaps not quite shattered with the collapse of the republic.

We are accustomed to thinking of the times going up like parchment in the fire in England during the Interregnum. We should extend the range, imagining, if we must have a revolution, the British rather than the English, visualising the Great British Rebellion, seeing 'the late troubles' as the products of all three kingdoms. Perhaps the best label to put on such complex events and developments, hard enough to interpret even if we confine our attention to England, would be 'The General Crisis of the British Isles'.

Notes

1. G. Holmes, 'The County Community in Stuart Historiography', Journal of British Studies, xix (1980), pp. 54–73.

2. I. Roots, 'Interest – Public, Private and Communal' in R.H. Parry (ed.), The English Civil War and After, 1642–1658 (1970), pp. 111–121 and The Late Troubles in England (Exeter, 1969).

3. See e.g. T.H. Aston (ed.), Crisis in Europe 1560–1660 (1965) and G. Parker and L.M. Smith (eds.), The General Crisis of the Seventeenth Century (1978).

4. E.S. Donno (ed.), Andrew Marvell: The Complete Poems (Harmondsworth, 1972), pp. 55–58, prints 'kingdoms' following E. Thompson's edition of The Works (1776). The British Library 1681 Miscellaneous Poems has 'kingdome'.

5. See Sir W.M. Petty, The Political Anatomy of Ireland (1691): 'That Carrickfergus may be always seen from Scotland is well known and but a small boat may row over in 3 or 4 hours is experienced' (p. 110). Irish historians have observed that Great Britain acted positively as 'a barrier between Ireland and the Continent' (e.g. J.C. Beckett, A Short History of Ireland (1968) p. 9). Petty saw the English as keeping 'the chain or drawbridge between the two kingdoms on the English side' (op. cit., p. 110). An M.P. in Richard Cromwell's parliament remarked that 'We are one clod of earth. Neptune lashes our shore on every side. We are as in a cockboat. We swim securely while we do not divide', J.T. Rutt (ed.), The Diary of Thomas Burton M.P., 4 vols. (1828), Vol. iv, p. 145. (Hereafter Burton's Diary).

6. G. Burnet, Memoires of the Dukes of the Hamilton (1677), Preface, Sig. a 2.

7. See W. Haller, Foxe's Book of Martyrs and the Elect Nation (1963).

8. A.H. Williamson, Scottish National Consciousness in the Age of James VI (Edinburgh, 1979), p. 15.

9. Williamson, op. cit., p. 145.

10. C.H. McIlwain (ed.), Political Works of James I (Cambridge, Mass., 1918), pp. 271–3.

11. See M. Lee, Jr., Government by the Pen: Scotland in the Reign of James VI and I (Urbana, 1980).

12. Polydore Vergil, Historia Anglia quoted in R.L. Mackie, King James IV of Scotland (Edinburgh, 1958), p. 93.

13. Charles II certainly thought the Covenant anti-monarchical: 'so long as this Covenant is in force....I have no more power in Scotland than as a Duke of Venice, which I will rather die than suffer'. Burnet, op. cit., pp. 59–61. See also W. Balcanquhal, A Large Declaration Concerning the Late Tumults in Scotland (1639). Cp. also Charles's answer to the 19 Propositions in 1642.

14. D. Stevenson, The Scottish Revolution 1637–44 (Newton Abbot, 1973), p. 57. 'Rebel' agents in London reported sympathy for the Covenant there. The Covenant was not in itself anti-English but opposed rule from England. Charles in fact had kept his English council, apart from a few like Laud, ignorant of his Scottish policies.

15. S.R. Gardiner, Constitutional Documents of the Puritan Revolution 1625–1660 (3rd ed. Oxford, 1906), pp. 199–201.

16. Williamson, op. cit., pp. 142–146.

17. See also W. Ferguson, Scotland's Relations with England: A Survey to 1707 (Edinburgh, 1977), p. 127, for the suggestion that there were hopes of a 'reformed international' exciting some interest on the continent. Archibald Johnson of Warington cited in G. Donaldson Scotland: James V – James VII (Edinburgh, 1978), p.332.

18. See e.g. V. Pearl, 'London's Counter-revolution' in G.E. Aylmer (ed.), The Interregnum (1972); her 'London Puritans and Scotch Fifth Columnists' in A.J. Hollaender and W. Kellaway, Studies in London History (1969); and D. Stevenson, Revolution and Counter-revolution in Scotland 1644-1651 (1977), esp. pp. 1–81.

19. Stevenson, op. cit., chapter 3 and 4. Charles agreed in the Engagement 'according to the intention of his father' to 'endeavour a complete union of the kingdoms, so as they may be one under his majesty', Gardiner op. cit., p. 351.

20. Stevenson, op. cit., p. 129.

21. C.H. Firth (ed.), The Cromwellian Union (Edinburgh, 1902), p. 6 n., quoting T. McCrie (ed.), The Life of Mr. Robert Blair (Woodrow Society, 1848), p. 291.

22. Firth, op. cit., pp. xvii and xxii. See also pp. xviii–xix for references to the need for union as for 'the good of this island' and for 'the good and peace of the people of this island'. C.H. Dand, The Mighty Affair: How Scotland lost her Parliament (Edinburgh, 1972), asserts per contra that 'all that Cromwell's total union of England and Scotland meant to the English was that the key of her back-door dangled safely from the Protector's belt' (p. 21).

23. Gardiner op. cit., p. 414, pp. 418-425. See also I. Roots, 'Cromwell's Ordinances' in G.E. Aylmer (ed.), The Interregnum (1972), pp. 156-8.

24. Gardiner op. cit., pp. 447-459; H. Scobell (ed.), A Collection of Acts and Ordinances (1658), pp. 389-395.

25. For the Debates see Burton's Diary, Vols. iii and iv, (reference to a 'treble-cord', Vol. iv, p. 7 and 168, 'provinces' and 'foreigners' Vol. iv, p. 130. E.D. Goldwater, 'The Scottish Franchise: Lobbying during the Cromwellian Protectorate', Historical Journal, xxi, (1978), pp. 27-42, brings out attitudes to the Scots in 1657.

26. C.H. Firth (ed.), The Memoirs of Edmund Ludlow, 2 vols. (Oxford, 1894), Vol. i, p. 298.

27. See the reports of Robert Lilburne in C.H. Firth (ed.), Scotland and the Commonwealth (Edinburgh, 1895), passim.

28. See F.D. Dow, Cromwellian Scotland 1651-1660 (Edinburgh, 1979), and esp. chapters 5-12, and M.P. Ashley, General Monck (1977), esp. chapters 9-15.

29. C.H. Firth, Cromwellian Union, Appendix of 'Papers relating to the Union Negotiations in 1670', pp. 187-224.

30. J. Swift, 'The Publick Spirit of the Whigs', in H. Davis (ed.), Political Tracts 1713-1714 (Oxford, 1953), p. 49.

31. See P. H. Scott (ed.), 1707: The Union of Scotland and England (Edinburgh, 1979), chapters 9 and 10 (pp. 55-67). H.R. Trevor-Roper (Religion, the Reformation and Social Change (1967), p. 466) sees the 1707 union as 'a revised version of the Cromwellian Union'.

32. See D.B. Quinn, The Elizabethans and the Irish (Ithaca, 1966), and N. Canny, The Elizabethan Conquest of Ireland 1565-1576 (1976), chapter 7.

33. See M. Perceval-Maxwell, The Scottish Migration to Ulster in the Reign of James I (1973).

34. See M. Perceval-Maxwell, 'Strafford, the Ulster-Scots and the Covenanters', I[rish] H[istorical] S[tudies], xviii (1972-3), pp. 524-551; H.F. Kearney, Strafford in Ireland (Manchester, 1959).

35. See M. Perceval-Maxwell, 'The Ulster Rebellion of 1641 and the Depositions', I.H.S., xxi (1978), pp. 144-167, esp. 155-165.

36. For reactions in England to the Rebellion see particularly K.S. Bottigheimer, English Money and Irish Land (Oxford, 1971), pp. 30-53 and K.J. Lindley, 'The Impact of the 1641 Rebellion upon England and Wales 1641-5', I.H.S., xviii (1972-3), pp. 143-176.

37. See J. Lowe, 'Charles I and the Confederation of Kilkenny 1643-9', I.H.S., xiv (1964), pp. 1-19.

38. See J.L. Malcolm, 'All the King's Men. The impact of the Crown's Irish soldiers on the English Civil War', I.H.S., xxii (1979), pp. 239-64. Malcolm cites John Lord Byron as representative of royalists who felt that since Parliament had called the Scots into England there was no reason 'Why the King should make any scruple of calling in the Irish, or the Turks if they would serve him'. See also Lindley op. cit., pp. 168-176.

39. The most recent account of the New Model Army is by H. Kishlansky, The Rise of the New Model Army (Cambridge, 1979). See also D. Massarella's article infra. H. Hazlett has surveyed 'The Financing of the British Armies in Ireland 1644-1649', I.H.S. (1935), pp.21-41. He notes a 'burst of activity' by Parliament in the late 1640s resulting in 'a simplified and more efficient way of bringing in its revenue' without which 'it is doubtful whether even Cromwell's military genius could have forced the decisive action he did in so short a time'. (p. 41).

40.
        And now the Irish are ashamed
        To see themselves in one year tamed:
          So much one man can do
          That does both act and know....
        He to the Commons' feet presents
        A kingdom for his first year's rent
          And what he may, forbears
          His fame, to make it theirs.
           (Donno, op. cit., pp. 56-7.)

41. See e.g. Firth, Ludlow's Memoirs, passim, and R.G., A Copy of a Letter from an Officer of the Army in Ireland to his Highness the Lord Protector (1656; reprint, Exeter 1974).

42. See T.C. Barnard, Cromwellian Ireland: English Government and Reform in Ireland 1649-1660 (Oxford, 1975), and 'Planters and Policies in Cromwellian Ireland', Past and Present, lxi (1973), pp. 31-69; and Dow, op. cit., pp. 161-228.

43. Bottigheimer op. cit., p. 3; M. MaCurtain, Tudor and Stuart Ireland (Dublin, 1972), pp. 154-160. For details of the Commonwealth Surveys see Y.M. Goblet, La transformation de la geographie politique de l'Irelande au XVIIe siècle (2 vols., Paris, 1930).

44. G.D. Owen (ed.), H.M.C. Report on the De L'Isle and Dudley MSS., Vol. vi (1966), pp. 596-9.

45. Burton's Diary, Vols. iii and iv, passim.

46. Quotes in Warner, op. cit., p. 575.

47. Bottigheimer, op. cit., p. 124.

48. Barnard, Cromwellian Ireland, p. 305. See also K. Bottigheimer, 'The Restoration Land Settlement in Ireland', I.H.S., xviii (1972) pp. 1-21.

2. Local Government Reform in England and Wales during the Interregnum : A Survey

STEPHEN ROBERTS

1. Civil War historians and the government of localities

The history of local government in mid-seventeenth century England and Wales has been something of a sacrifice to historiographical conflict. It is a problem which has attracted interest only since the turn of the century and its slender bibliography has endowed it with little resistance to grander themes. Macaulay was interested in local matters only as a backcloth to an epic and even S.R. Gardiner, penetrating as all his judgments were, offered no interpretation of local institutional change. J.R. Tanner, it is true, considered the justice of the peace but only as a monument to Tudor 'constructive genius', as a symptom of a 'centralised administration'. Early socialist historians took up the theme of the centralised state as a check on the local landed gentry, whose innate acquisitiveness would naturally break forth at any opportunity. E.M. Leonard described the endeavours of Laud and Strafford in the field of poor relief as

> remarkable for more continuous effort to enforce socialistic measures than has been made by the central government of any other great European country.[1]

The 'Puritan Revolution', by contrast, was a victory for bourgeois self-interest. Suspicion of local oligarchies, one presumes, would not have been shared by the great nineteenth-century Liberals, for whom 'local self-government' was a watchword elevated to a political philosophy. Macaulay, after all, had reluctantly condemned the Protectorate as a despotism 'moderated only by the wisdom, the sobriety and the magnanimity of the despot'.[2] There might be differences over whether local self-government was or was not beneficial, but socialists and Whigs could broadly agree that local government was under the control of the centralised state until the civil war, when collapse was succeeded by relaxed central supervision.

More recently, those who have studied local administration directly have endorsed the findings of Sidney and Beatrice Webb who emphasised the tightened grip of J.P.s on county institutions.

This interpretation, with its respectable if short-lived pedigree, was accommodated by later views. Trevor-Roper's 'revolt of the provinces' against a centralising Renaissance monarchy accords well with a view of 1660 as making no significant difference to the relationship between 'the State' and 'society'. Central government control was over and had been ended probably in 1641. However stimulating Trevor-Roper's work, it needed to be substantiated by more local research and it was Alan Everitt who took up the theme of 'centralisation', reversed it and introduced the concept of an England before the civil war as a federation of 'county communities', provoked into war by the ineptitude and successive encroachments of Charles I and his ministers. For Everitt the Commonwealth and Protectorate were simply part of 'a series of centralising governments', in David Underdown's words.[3] Underdown himself has seen in the Protectorate not fully-blown centralisation, but forces tending to accommodation with the localities, to 'settlement' and to centralisation, each striving for mastery in the country, and each personified in the character and aims of Oliver Cromwell himself.

These debates over the significance of the civil war in the localities have, on the whole, eschewed the study of local institutions. The intrusive county committees are the exception but their significance has been over-stated; they were reformed in the early 1650s and the remaining militia and assessments committees were hardly more powerful than the early Stuart subsidy and lieutenancy commissions. No-one could deny that county committees injected a measure of central direction into local affairs; more than that, they were in some places the only institution, once war had broken out, between the localities and anarchy. The concept of the 'county community' as the expression of gentry power has been fought both for and against but these battles have naturally been focussed on the 1640s. We await Dr. Morrill's sequel to The Revolt of the Provinces: Conservatives and Radicals in the English Civil War 1630-1650 but his researches into the history of Cheshire during the Interregnum suggest that he considers the extension of initiatives at parish level to be one important feature of the reconstruction. The Interregnum has been treated most directly by David Underdown whose Pride's Purge and essay on 'Settlement in the Counties' have surveyed the Commonwealth and Protectorate broadly but with great insight. The emphasis has, however, been more on personnel than on structure, more on participation than on performance.

'Centralisation' has been the key in debates on changes in local government. Everitt and Underdown would agree that 'revolutionary governments are usually centralising governments' and would differ only on the extent of the process. But it is not simply a question of how far 'centralisation' qua 'alienation-of-the-gentry' was allowed to proceed. Here are some random examples of how inadequate the concept of the centralising state could be. In Glamorgan, the county committee, originally the agent of Whitehall, became impenetrable to outside authority and became a bulwark of localism. The excise regulations of the Rump developed formal administrative procedures but involved devolution to local officeholders on a scale significant enough to allow Sir Roger Twysden of Kent to make payment arrangements with the excise office largely on his own terms. Major-Generals James Berry and Robert Lilburne found that excisemen were deviant localists and implored Secretary Thurloe to 'be careful in disposing powers and places to put them into good hands or you undo us'. Finally in Cheshire we find the 'godly', including ministers intruded by central committee, establishing parish vestries to increase local administrative initiatives on, for example, alehouse reform. We might do well to heed the apposite (but not succinct) words of a specialist on modern bureaucracies:

> A realistic analysis of centralisation must
> include a study of the allocation of decisions in
> the organisation and the methods of influence
> that are employed by the higher levels to affect
> the decisions at the lower levels.[4]

The 'methods of influence' used by central governments in the 1650s are still unstudied. Professor Roots's comment in 1972 that work on how ordinances were implemented 'has hardly been attempted' remains true in 1981.[5]

Contemporaries would not have understood the term 'centralisation' in our sense. This is not to imply that the concept is necessarily invalid, of course: Oliver Cromwell would have puzzled to learn that he led a 'bourgeois revolution' but modern historians have found that idea useful in revaluing the 'Great Rebellion'. But what does have considerable import is the apparent lack of a mid-seventeenth century notion of 'local government'. Most historians have assumed a dichotomy in government between central and local matters, and the commission of the peace is generally used as a frontier of local government vis-à-vis the centre. There might, however, be reason to doubt these assumptions.

The fact that the Oxford English Dictionary finds no usage of 'local' as meaning 'pertaining to a particular locality', as against 'central', before 1688 – and that a New England usage – is not necessarily a difficulty. What is more striking is the consensus among political theorists about the shared responsibilities of government and governed which attached no significance to local rights or independence. Men spoke figuratively of 'commonwealths' at the most intimately local levels. Sir Thomas Smith described parish government as for 'men which doe not rule', and John Norden wrote that a manor was a 'little commonwealth whereof the tenants...are the members, the land the body and the lord the head'.[6] They spoke with some justification since customary law was that which influenced the lives of ordinary people most directly, and at least one historian considers that local self-government was real enough since 'early by-laws proceed from the farming community rather than from the lord of the manor'.[7] But any initiatives in this world are enjoyed by the yeomanry, not by the political and social elites of the 'county community'.

Such views blend with 'Country' perceptions of the corruptions of the Court expressed in the 'country house' poetry of Ben Jonson and Andrew Marvell and the classical pastoral of Milton. Whether they amount to a political philosophy in any positive sense is very doubtful indeed. The dominant view of the body politic was that expounded by Sir Thomas Wentworth in his speech to the Council of the North in December 1628. He stressed the 'joint individual well-being of sovereignty and subjection' and made no distinction between the local and central aspects of government. His insistence that 'distemper'd minds have of late very farr endeavoured to divide the consideracions of the two' was an attack on those who had allegedly confused 'private fortune' with the public good, not a comment on a wayward localism. His views were, at the level of political debate, unexceptionable. The historians who have written about the 'revolt of the provinces' have shown how conservative and how pragmatic the local response to the civil war was. This is not to deny the validity of the central/local split, or to wish away the civil war itself, but simply to argue for a lack of contemporary ideological basis for 'county' localism.

2. Proposals for the reform of local administration

Constitutional discussions and proposals from 1647 to 1649 touched upon local government, albeit indirectly as a consequence of the view that the centralised state should be dismantled. The army 'grandees' suggested in the 'Heads of the Proposals' of August 1647 an element of popular election in the localities, although institutions were to remain unchanged. Justices of the peace were to be elected by grand jurors, themselves chosen in freeholders' meetings, and the King was to choose a sheriff from the three candidates nominated by the jurors of each county. The Levellers, particularly John Lilburne and Richard Overton, addressed the question more directly. They sought a complete reversal of the pattern of accountability by officials to superiors; election 'by the people in their respective places' was to be the new guiding rule. The parish was to be not only the basic unit of government but was to recover an administrative and political integrity which, according to the Levellers, it had lost at the Norman Conquest. There were to be courts in each hundred, consisting of elected jurors. All local officials were to be elected for a term of one year only. Tax assessors were to be elective. Their plans amounted to 'a blue-print for a society of self-governing communities, with a large degree of voluntaryism'.[8] Dr. Manning holds that the Levellers faltered and failed to press these proposals and that their uncertainty cost them political success, but the radicalism of their conception of local autonomy was an impediment in their campaign for acceptance of the Agreements of the People. Their views ran against an almost universal acceptance of authoritarian, paternalistic notions of government as the shared responsibility of governors and governed, of 'central' and 'local' authorities. The Levellers wanted more than 'devolution' or 'decentralisation'; they sought a flow of power from the parishes out-wards which would leave the central authority at the furthest (and weakest) point of its scope.

The Levellers' idea of the primacy of each community percolated into later debates on law reform, as we shall discover, but their emphasis on political change was unique in exposing the injustice of how constitutional arrangements discriminated in favour of a wealthy and powerful oligarchy. Gerrard Winstanley perceived the fundamental injustice to be the ownership of property, and proposed in The Law of Freedom in a Platform, his most mature work, that issues of government would be settled by attention to the basis of relationships between individuals. There is an emphasis in Digger writings on the tasks of local governors, on their personal carriage, which is not to be found among the Levellers. Winstanley started from the premise that

> All...offices are like links of a chain, they
> arise from one and the same root, which is
> necessity of common peace...

but apart from asserting the need for popular election of all officers, he offers no developed view of political democracy.

Those two most enduringly influential philosophers of the English Revolution, Hobbes and Harrington, have nothing of great moment to say about local government. Leviathan's power is indivisible, or at least there is to be allowed only such freedoms as he thinks fit. As

Charles Blitzer points out, Harrington's _Oceana_ leaves many responsibilities to local officials but he is surely mistaken to describe
these as 'decentralisation'; Oceana's tax-collecting arrangements were
those of early Stuart, 'centralised state', England.[9]

The Levellers were the only political thinkers of the English
Revolution to devise a notion of 'local government' as the basis of
political change. Their defeat in 1649 did not bury ideas of 'decentralisation' however: their standard passed to a group of radical lawyers,
who as a pressure group in the Rump and in the Nominated Assembly came
nearer to success than the Levellers had ever done, if success is to be
judged in legislative achievement.

As both judicial and administrative tasks were the
responsibilty of local courts, law reformers can be viewed as local
government reformers too, even though the burden of their demands
emphasised codification of the criminal law. As in contemporary New
England

> law reform could not occur without a concomitant
> reformation of social institutions, economic
> conditions and political processes.[10]

And yet it seems that the radical lawyers thought it could, or thought
at least that wider reform could be severely limited. The Leveller
notion of county courts re-appears in the deliberations of the Hale
Commission in 1652 and surfaced in a draft of a bill during Barebone's
Parliament. The county judicatures would prevent

> unnecessary charge and delay in recovering of
> rights by the course of the common law.[11]

Mary Cotterell has argued that these courts were by no means independent
of central control; they would have been outposts of the Courts of
Common Pleas and the judges would not have been elected. Matthew Hale
himself wanted to restore Common Pleas to primacy in civil cases against
the unwelcome competition from King's Bench (or Upper Bench as it was
during the 1650s). The Hale Commission is more evidence of a common
lawyers' feud than of Leveller sympathies.

The lawyers confined themselves to procedural change, and did
not propose extensive innovation in the common law itself. It is not
surprising, however, that critics of the Hale Commission should have
attributed to it more radical aims than those it actually espoused.
After all, even if county judcatures were to be supervised from the
centre, their very existence would have threatened the primacy of courts
of quarter sessions in each county. Although they may best be considered as local branches of Common Pleas, the county courts would have
dealt with 'all criminal matters' as well, and could have driven a wedge
between the judicial and administrative powers of magistrates. Critics
saw the dangers to the State and attacked notions of county autonomy:

> The interests of Rigths [sic] and Priviledges of
> each county...will protect malefactors and stop
> the whole Course of Justice; our own experience
> manifests the truth in the Courts of the Marches
> of Wales and the North...In each county the
> Judges will expound the Rule according to the
> several Interests in the Counties...so many
> Judicatories, so many several Laws.[12]

Here the argument of central versus local is laid bare; this is a rebuff
to the Levellers as well as to the Hale Commission, and its tenor would
have been echoed by Oliver Cromwell, enthusiast of legal reform though
he was.

These sorts of proposals were consistently unpopular, if
persistent in duration. They were usually associated with calls for
county land registries. Henry VIII had intended these in the Statute of
Enrolments of 1535 but the spirit if not the letter of the act had been
flouted by common lawyers, who, to satisfy the demands of the propertied
for secrecy in their transactions, had invented the collusive rigmaroles
of fines and recoveries. Calls for land registries appeared in 1646 and
later brought the business of the Rump to a standstill, appeared once
more in 1653, again in the second Protectorate Parliament, in William
Sheppard's England's Balme of 1656 and in a curtain-call in 1659 in
Chaos, by a Well-Willer to the Common Weal. Nothing concrete was
achieved during the Interregnum, but some of the schemes, especially
those of Barebones' Parliament, were worked out down to the details of
office hours and the kind of ledger to be used. The argument for land
registries was that 'every man may see what is his and what is
another's'; the argument against was that they would unduly bolster the
power of the State, whether centralised or 'cantonised':

> Thus may the State be intituled to most of the
> lands in England; hence also will the Common-
> wealth swarm with Informers, Prowlers and
> Searchers into others Titles.[13]

3. The interrelationship of central and local government

To summarise thus far: the consensus of opinion in mid-
seventeenth century England was that government was a matter of shared
rights and obligations, to be interpreted by each subject according to
his social position. There was no concept of boundaries between central
and local responsibilities and no recognition that the rights of local
governors could differ fundamentally from those of men in Whitehall (who
were, in any case, also men of their own counties). The only concept of
'local government' which would have been acknowledged before the mid-
1640s, before the appearance of county committees, would have been that
of parish government and in a more restricted sense, of manorial
government, in which rights and obligations to the outside were minimal.
Thus the advocacy by the Levellers of a reversed flow of obligations was
strikingly original and it is not surprising that it stimulated other
radicals and provoked opposition. The reforming lawyers seized on
Leveller proposals for county judicatures and accommodated them into

their own more cautious schemes for the reform of procedure; during the
Interregnum change in local government structures was discussed only as
an aspect of wider legal reform; there was no recognizable 'local
government reform' lobby.

The Interregnum was, however, a legislatively fruitful decade
and even if local institutions emerged largely unscathed at the end of
it because there was no political will to alter them, it is worth
looking for patterns which might emerge from the legislative
achievement. Was it true that central control was slackened?

It must be recognized that acts of Parliament (and
Protectoral ordinances) could be passed to satisfy local and specific
interest groups, and that each statute should properly be examined in
the light of pressure brought to bear on Westiminster and Whitehall for
and against it. The act against adultery and fornication, of 1650, and
the Navigation Act of 1651 are considered by some to be the fruits of
pressure – group politics; in the first case by Puritan ministers of the
City of London, in the second by interloping free trade merchants. But
those who would argue that it may not always be helpful to emphasise the
stop-gap and the pragmatic in legislation may be succoured by Mr.
Thomas's proof that the 1650 act was the culmination of a century-long
interest at Westminster in repression, and Mr. Cooper's view that outside lobbying had nothing to do with the Navigation Act. There is a
corpus of Interregnum legislation relating to local matters and it would
be helpful to study it for any consistent trends or drifts, however
inconsistent or ambivalent its origins and apparent purposes.

The principal organs of county government remained unaltered
from the 1630s through to 1660, and indeed Lambarde's _Eirenarcha_ of 1582
can be used with the Webbs' account of local government after 1688 to
piece together the duties and avenues of responsibility. Sheriffs
waited on the judges of assize, were held liable for certain Crown, and
later State, revenues and accounted to the Exchequer for them. Clerks
of the peace were appointed by the custos rotulorum, who was primus
inter pares of the Bench of magistrates. The justices themselves were
responsible to the Lord Keeper under the monarchy and during the
Interregnum to Parliament and subsequently to the Council of State.
High constables were usually appointed at quarter sessions; petty constables in a bewilderingly wide variety of ways germane to their own
parishes and manors.

(a) The Sheriff

The Interregnum shrievalty exemplified the contradictions of
'settlement' and control, of how close to home governments had to fight
a campaign of inducement and intimidation. Judge Francis Thorpe's
charge to the assizes at York in March 1649 was, as charges always were,
a propaganda exercise on behalf of the government, but it contained a
profoundly conservative description of local obligations. Dearth had to
be relieved by punishing middlemen, and weights and measures laws had to
be enforced. The one passage in which Thorpe strayed from the Tudor/
early Stuart orthodox, not to say commonplace, was in a discussion of
the shrievalty:

This is a great officer and is much trusted in
the service of the people and by the state of
articulum super chartas, is to be chosen yearly
by the people, that they might the better be
assured of those they trusted. But this privi-
lege of election (among others) the people have
lost and the court, of later times, did learn how
to make profit, both by electing sheriffs, as
also by keeping them off from being elected.[14]

The sheriff was the only elected official in Thorpe's catalogue; that in
practice he was the most accountable to a department of government, the
Exchequer, indicates the Judge's sanguine insistence on the popular
basis of the Commonwealth: such a bold inversion of what was commonly
observable suggests a degree of confidence by Thorpe which the later
history of the Interregnum did nothing to justify. There was never any
popular election of sheriffs and the difficulty encountered throughout
the decade in finding reliable and willing men was partly a result of
popular alienation, as well as a comment on the increasing burden of the
office. In Warwickshire between 1647 and 1658 only four of the fourteen
sheriffs were identifiable Parliamentarians; in Glamorgan there were
absentees; in other counties, including Kent, there were sheriffs who
had been royalists.

The difficulties in securing a reliable shrievalty became
critical during the interlude of the major-generals. The new militia,
to act as a 'quick-sett hedge' for security, was to be paid for by the
enemies of the State, and had to be supervised in each county by an
official. The sheriff seemed the obvious choice. From November 1655 to
January 1656 the major-generals tried to select suitable sheriffs from
lists of two or three candidates sent to them by the Council of State.
They immediately fell into the localist trap: the best man for the job
should not be so badly treated as to be submitted to its expense.
Major-General Berry cynically described the choice in one of the Welsh
border counties:

Mr. Turvey is good for little; a rich clowne that
would be glad to be taken notice of, and perhaps
might be ruled. Mr. Foley you all know, yet for
his own sake I wish he might be spared, for the
saying is here, that a man had as good be se-
questered as made sherife.[15]

Even in more settled times, the office had been regarded as
an onerous and (more importantly) as an expensive imposition. Much of
the expense was incurred in entertaining judges and juries at assizes.
J.S. Cockburn considers it 'obvious' that sheriffs 'were habitually
open-handed at assize time'[16] but fails to square this with the
resentment, the dread, which the call to office could invoke. More
research would probably confirm that a generous scale of hospitality was
institutionalised or built into the sheriff's duties. The other burden
was that of supervising tax collection. Here the shrievalty had been
discredited as the agency for ship-money; to be useful once more the
office called for rehabilitation. An early act of the Rump allowed
sheriffs their expenses in passing accounts but qualified this gen-
erosity in July 1650 by making sheriffs accountable for the distribution

of all enacted legislation. (The easing of fees on owners of liberties
the same year may appear as relief for those charged with collecting
them, the sheriffs, but was really designed to make the purchase of confiscated lands more attractive.) Sheriffs were never reliable enough to
be entrusted with the collection of the monthly assessments (which
increased in Bedfordshire, for example, by over one third between 1649
and 1652); they were left to receivers-general, usually soldiers, in
each county.

The major-generals were left to correct the casual and
inconsistent attitudes towards sheriffs of earlier governments of the
1650s. To excuse their friends from the office was to acknowledge that
they were helpless. (After the major-generals had been voted down, it
could be noted frankly in Parliament that if the royalists were excluded
from all offices, 'you will have neither sheriffs nor constables'.[17])
The major-generals chose instead to alter the pattern of appointments.
In most of the counties of England and Wales there were only two or
perhaps three appointments between 1655 and 1660 when there should have
been five or six. Men acceptable to the government were found and then
kept in office. These five years saw fewer appointments to the shrievalty than at any other time in the century. This despite the triumph of
conservatism in central accounting procedures. Attempts to reduce the
finances of the Commonwealth and Protectorate 'to one Treasury' had been
frequent since the disbanding of the county committees in 1650. The
victory of the Exchequer over the Treasury in 1654 has been viewed as
evidence of the regime's conservatism, but the way in which the central
court of the Exchequer and its old servants, the sheriffs, became separ-
ated suggests at least a spark of radicalism. The unity of the
Exchequer, in London and in the counties, had been broken.

(b) The jury

The shrievalty was thus an organ of local government which
did receive legislative attention, unlike the commissions of the peace
which were merely re-staffed as it became necessary. The jury system,
too, was addressed directly. Briefly, juries, like justices, fulfilled
an administrative as well as a judicial role. At assizes and quarter
sessions they were to present offences, that is, to bring to the
attention of the courts defects in roads and bridges, lapses in social
obligations, both by communities and by individuals, as well as un-
covered criminal offences. Schemes for the reform of juries centred on
the compilation of accurate lists of freeholders so that no-one of
insufficient wealth or social standing could be impanelled. This task
became more pressing in the aftermath of the civil wars; a jury of
royalist sympathisers, (or, after 1653, of Commonwealth sympathisers,
not to mention presbyterian partisans) could wreak havoc with official
views of local justice, seen by most to be at the 'bowels' of the common
weal. From the early 1650s, orders at quarter sessions were made for
the listing of freeholders; a general order was sent to all the counties
of the Western Circuit in 1648. In fact there had been complaints of
'insufficient' [i.e., inadequate in quality] juries from places as far
apart as Devon and East Anglia as early as the 1610s, but in the 1640s
and 50s the problem was taken up by the radical lawyers and found a
solution in one of the proposed Barebones' statutes. The orders do not
seem to have borne fruit in the areas where they have been studied; as
with the deficiencies in the shrievalty it was left to the major-
generals to tackle the problems with any gusto. Possibly as a result of

pressures brought to bear upon him by the Devon bench of magistrates, Oliver Cromwell wrote to the major-generals in January 1656. He spoke, characteristically, of the way in which the weak suffered at the hands of the 'subtle' who were insinuating themselves on to jury panels.[18] Here routine administration and his beloved 'reformation of manners' could meet.

Cromwell proposed the expedient of listing; the major-generals received the message each according to his own temperament. Disbrowe and Whalley were pessimistic; Worsley was, as ever, enthusiastic; Goffe asserted that this prosaic task of registration 'very much rejoyceth the people'.[19] Its effects were, as far as we can tell, as short-lived as the major-generals' campaign itself. Most historians seem agreed that the jury system was, in any case, a ground-less worry; it displayed no independence and could easily be bullied into submission. It was simply an aspect of a general concern for security. The only flash of initiative among juries has been noted by J.S. Morrill in Cheshire; as well as frequently criticising the magis-trates the jury on a number of occasions nominated new justices. There are several peculiarities about administration in Cheshire, however; first, as a county palatine it was never visited by a circuit judge. Instead the county fell under the influence of John Bradshaw, who had presided at the trial of Charles I and who was Chief Justice of Chester. Secondly, the nominations and criticisms offered by the jury were all made at assizes, the court most directly under Bradshaw's control. Finally, there is evidence from a nearby Welsh county to support the view that Bradshaw manipulated the jury for his own purposes. In the summer of 1656, when the major-generals were campaigning to secure their sympathisers for the second Protectorate Parliament (and to exclude Bradshaw), the Flintshire jury suggested nine new men as justices. They were all moderate county gentry and the careers of two as Rump committeemen had coincided with Bradshaw's period as President of the Council of State. Bradshaw presided over the Court of Great Sessions in Wales and as the year 1656 was marked by his contretemps with Cromwell it seems more than coincidence that the Flintshire jury should suddenly erupt at the same time. The history of the institution both in Cheshire and in North Wales seems to prove simply that the jury was the property of whoever could control it.

The fortunes of trial by jury have been read as a measure of administrative radicalism during the civil war. Parliament relied heavily on the committee 'system' which by-passed the need for popular consent, and perhaps as significantly, obviated the need for extensive control. 'No ordinance between 1642-6 required the impannelling of juries.'[20] The 'middling sort' were denied their traditional voice in those years; should we regard the return to the jury in the legislation of the Protectorate as a belated victory of the freeholders? The new committees of 'judges' appointed to relieve 'poor prisoners' (debtors) under Barebones was amended in 1654 to include a rôle for juries, but the emphasis during the 1650s was, as we have seen, on control; there is no evidence of any local initiatives to recover the rights of free juries, nor any enhancement of their duties in a new framework of local government.

(c) The constable

At lower levels of local government participation, there were no significant changes in conditions or duties. There were increasing refusals by constables to take office but this was to be expected in a period of increasing central taxation. Not only were constables charged with the collection of the monthly assessment; after August 1649 they were called upon to collect the excise as well. There can be no doubt that the excise was an extremely unpopular tax, but its emergence should not be regarded as a simple act of centralisation. Certainly it was viewed by taxpayers as an unwarranted interference with 'liberties' but administrators of the excise were seen in different lights by different observers. Excisemen could be localists. One feature of the increased work-load of constables was that they could argue, in negotiations with their 'employers' at quarter sessions, that they were on the business of 'the State', as did the constables of Lancashire in 1652. But a general account of the office of constable must await future research; at present we are unable to distinguish overall patterns from the particular conditions of each county.

(d) Centralisation or interference?

Those institutions directly tackled by central government were not the victims of 'centralisation', therefore, but were simply 'interfered with', in campaigns to secure the safety of the State as a whole, and to improve public finance. The 'centralisation' case is weakened still further if assizes and quarter sessions courts are considered. The former were used by the Commonwealth to secure consent to the political changes upon which it was founded, but assizes never again fulfilled the rôle of local government inspectorate which the early Stuarts had assigned to them. Assizes were inseparably associated with 'Thorough'. At quarter sessions 'angling for support' continued all through the Interregnum and changes in the commissions of the peace should not be taken as changes in the local power structure. Many were national changes only, especially those of the early 1650s.

Local performance in administration held up well during the Interregnum. No-one now believes that poor relief collapsed during the decade because of some dour 'Puritan work ethic' which doomed the poor to self-help or starvation. Research on regions as diverse as Yorkshire, Cheshire, Warwickshire, Devon, Shropshire and London all confirm that magistrates met their responsibilities squarely, if not always imaginatively. The pattern of relief varied considerably but the problem confronting local governors was one of money not of will. This could take several forms. In Devon it appeared as a series of imaginative orders at quarter sessions which, even after a torrent of vituperative attacks on defaulting accountants, ended in 1660 with virtually nothing accomplished. In London, finance was the greatest difficulty facing the governors of the new workhouse. By the later 1650s, these problems had produced new remedies. In Devon, Essex and Warwickshire there were moves towards the appointment of overall county treasurers, and in Cheshire a single county rate for all bridge repairs was planned. Unified county funding would have been hastened by an act of 1657 which stipulated that a separate rate for road repairs should be levied. It marked a shift away from labour towards fiscal obligations upon parishioners. In Hertfordshire the justices took over the funds of the disbanded militia bureaucracy for poor relief and other county purposes. There was a blurred image in the localities of a national drift away from fees towards salaries for officials, too.

It has been argued that there was no specific lobby for local government reform after the defeat of the Levellers, except where the plans of the radical lawyers for structural change touched upon it en passant. Changes were made ad hoc, and were a low priority except where they affected the physical and fiscal security of government. Interregnum legislation bore upon the conduct of everyday life in the provinces but it is remarkable how little of it - occupying 700 pages of Acts and Ordinances of the Interregnum - altered the procedures of local administration.

6. Central government agencies in the localities

If government enhanced its powers, its knowledge of local events, it did so not through the local courts but through central government agencies with outposts in the localities: the post office, the customs and excise offices, and, of course, the army and the establishments of the major-generals.

(a) The Post Office

There was nothing new in governments trying to monitor the movement of population. Tudor statutes on alehouse control, for example, included injunctions to constables to inform magistrates of new arrivals in their parishes. Edmund Prideaux, postmaster-general from 1644 to 1653, developed the institution as an agency for government intelligence; Thomas Edwards, in Gangraena, indignantly chronicled outrages by the Independents in opening mail to and from London. Under the Rump this continued unchecked. From 1651 there were alternative schemes for farming the service; one was espoused by Thomas Pride and City of London radicals in an effort to oust Edmund Prideaux, no ally of theirs. The decision to farm was eventually taken under Barebones.

Senior postal officers bitterly opposed the decision. In a reversal of the early Stuart pattern, in which members of parliament had volubly upheld the 'public good' against self-interested courtiers and monopolists, the officials argued that this parliamentary decision would allow private interests to prevail over public, and would forfeit the goodwill of the 'godly' (reliable) in the provinces. To scotch the scheme they even offered to guarantee a higher annual profit to the government, if necessary out of their own pockets, than the farmers were to return. They spoke for 'all the godly and well-affected postmasters'[21] and, as their own positions were not threatened, there is little reason to doubt them. After the Restoration the post office was considered to be a notorious refuge for adherents of the 'Good Old Cause'. So why farm? The timing of the decision, when radicalism was at a zenith in Parliament, suggests a victory for the opponents of the conservative, presbyterian Prideaux, and a radical government might be anxious to play down the significance of the office as an intelligence bureau. Certainly the legislation establishing the farm in September 1654 studiously avoided any reference to this side of the work. Preliminary instructions by the farmer, Captain John Manley, did include provisions for noting the names of travellers and guests at inns. These activities were to be kept secret, even though most people must have realised that postmasters had long been concerned in these matters. Even Gerrard Winstanley, of all people, thought that postmasters should inform governments of local events.

Manley's farm ran for an appointed two years but was not renewed. A committee chaired by Philip Jones, one of Cromwell's most trusted administrators, advised that the postal service should be 'farmed' to John Thurloe. This was a victory for the intelligence service. After the Restoration one observer remembered that

> Another great intrigue of Cromwell was carefully
> to watch the Generall letter Office....for
> through this Office are conveyed all the poy-
> sonous distempers of the Citty into the whole
> Kingdome....[22]

Letters had been intercepted before, of course, but Cromwell employed one man, Isaac Dorislaus, to undertake this task. In an ordinance of June 1657, which strengthened government control over the post office, once of the functions of the office was declared to be

> to discover and prevent many dangerous and wicked
> designs which have been and are daily contrived
> against the Peace and Welfare of this Common-
> wealth.[23]

One of the strengths of Interregnum governments was the quiet progress in home intelligence which enabled the plots of royalists and others to be nipped in the bud. The population was undoubtedly observed more closely but the enumeration of guests at inns was restrained, undertaken by postal officials who were self-effacing men about whom little is known. They were supported by local customs-house officers who, during the 1650s, were usually military men. 'Centralisation', if it means anything in this period, means the acquisition by government of a more finely-tuned awareness of the behaviour of citizens.

(b) The registry

Postmasters were scrutinized by the major-generals in one of the highest priorities of their campaign, which began in the autumn of 1655. It was the aftermath of Penruddock's rising and at the heart of the instructions to the major-generals was a new means of observing the movement of population. In October a registry for the depositing of bonds taken from suspects was established. The procedures were elaborate and involved a double system of registration, to survey the movements of the disaffected and the innocent householder on the move. Secretary Thurloe was slow to execute the instructions of the Council as they touched upon the registry. In December Thomas Dunn was appointed as the registrar in London. His duties, office hours and even the number of ledgers he was to keep, were all stipulated. By then the major-generals were inquiring, some rather tetchily, into the delays in introducing the scheme. Between January and April 1656 Dunn was hampered by his failure to secure suitable office accommodation in

London, but he received no help from his employers. Despite these set-
backs, Dunn sent out letters and printed forms to the major-generals on
1 January 1656 and soon the completed bonds began to return.

The registration plan has been attacked as 'too grand-
iose'[24] but it seemed to work adequately. The decimation tax, the
meddling with juries and, above all, the lack of interested supervision
from the centre provoked anguished outbursts from the major-generals;
the taking of bonds, 'to which soe much of our work relates', went com-
paratively smoothly. The letter books and the volumes of suspects'
names suggest efficiency not _folie de grandeur_. Of course there were
problems, partly over Dunn's London address but chiefly in ensuring that
travellers turned up at the office. Nevertheless, the system worked
well enough to note the eighteen moves made by John Turner of
Bletchingley in Surrey, the eleven journeys of Simon Heveningham of
Richmond and the eight trips of Nicholas Borlase of Newlyn, Cornwall -
all during 1656.

Disbrowe's sub-commissioners in Wiltshire, Dorset, Devon,
Cornwall, Somerset and Gloucester took bonds from over 5,000 people.
Their names were recorded, in alphabetical order, in one of Thomas
Dunn's fat ledgers. The occupation or style of each was given,
according to the instructions to the sub-commissioners by Disbrowe and
Dunn. The lists were by no means simply a roll-call of ex-royalist
delinquents. Rural tradesmen and county and parish gentry were all
scrutinized, and if the homes of the Devon suspects are plotted on a map
it appears that registration was most intense where the population was
most concentrated, rather than where most of the royalists were. The
registry worked in accordance with principles of administration, in
other words, as well as with the political principles of its masters.
Although the major-generals were voted down in Parliament on 28 January
1657 the registry continued to operate until April, and the last foreign
suspect was registered on 10 August.

The major-generals' registry was apparently inspired by John
Lambert, but the concept and scope of the institution echoed several
earlier themes of the Interregnum. Comprehensive listing had been
associated with jury control and with plans for land registries. The
need for comprehensive information was being recognized, and more
importantly, seemed almost within the capacity of governments. The
wider demands for security had been obvious in reforms in the post
office and in the continued presence of the army. The major-generals
and their registry were the civil and military aspects of security
apotheosised together. The regulation of personal conduct, too, had a
respectable pedigree before the men on horseback took up the challenge.
Sexual offences, blasphemy, cock-fighting, race-meetings, swearing among
dockers had all been attacked before 1655. What was new about the experiment was not its methods or its personnel but the principles behind
it. It was a surrender to a hard-pressed minority in the counties who
had borne 'the heat of the day'; it was an acknowledgment that their
interests and those of others were not the same. The most enthusiasm
for the scheme was evinced not by the major-generals themselves but by
their subordinate commisssioners in each county, who regarded themselves
as a minority and who did not pretend to have public opinion on their
side. They would have endorsed the sentiments of the Yorkshire
cavalier, Sir John Gibson:

The Decimation of my 'state
'Tis not worth valuation;
I fear 'twill prove a common fate
To all of this same Nation.[25]

(c) The major-generals

The impact of the major-generals, and indeed that of the
other regimes of the Interregnum, upon the parishes of England and Wales
has been unwarrantably neglected. We know something of parochial initiatives in government, of how in some places the select vestry emerges
from the later 1640s onwards as a bulwark against anarchy in rural
communities. Committees of 'ministers and the better sort' licensed
alehouses in Cheshire. The same 'middling sort' approval had to be
found to obtain an alehouse licence in Exeter during the 1650s, and in
the counties of Wiltshire, Worcestershire and Somerset. But at the same
time there emerged, in some counties, in some parishes, a contrary
symptom of enhanced power by magistrates. The campaign by Thomas
Delavell, J.P., in Houghton-le-Spring, County Durham, is an example.
From the early 1650s Delavell supervised the activities of churchwardens
and constables and annually scrutinized their accounts. Inspired by the
publication of Henry Scobell's A Collection of Acts and Ordinances, in
1658, he wrote up the procedures to be followed by parish officials in
their many aspects.

Elsewhere, there is evidence from the mid-1650s that
magistrates were taking a greater interest in parish administration,
evidence that cannot, for the most part, be related to the activities of
the major-generals. There was an increasing spread of political
participation which comprehended magistrates, churchwardens and major-
generals' commissioners. Occasionally there was blatant interference,
particularly in the boroughs before the elections to the second
Protectorate Parliament. It could take the form of heavy-handed moral
censure. Martin Pyke distributed fines taken from swearers and
drunkards, to the poor of Hastings in 1656. Pyke was a Kentish man, so
was both an outsider and a trespasser against local preferences for
harmony not divisiveness. The weakening of determined reluctance to
participate in government may be taken as a sign that a measure of
political stability was returning under the Protectorate. By the 1670s
parish vestries of the 'middling sort' and the petty sessions of the
magistrates had both become unexceptional aspects of local government.

It was a lack of politcal support, either from the Protector
or from Parliament which brought down the major-generals. But some have
detected a lack of central enthusiasm for the scheme from its beginning,
at least among civilian administrators like Thurloe. Cromwell himself
was more interested in moral reformation than in the details of bureaucratic control. The episode of the major-generals certainly reveals the
limitations of government, in the physical sense. Failures of communi-
cation were rife; difficulties over finance were a variation on this
theme, as well. The major-generals and their registry were just an echo
of committee government in the 1640s, in which there were no procedural
rules, but simply a series of accretions, of ad hoc decisions accumu-
lating to form their own frame of reference. The government was trying
to operate on the frontiers of procedural possibility and it is difficult to see how it could have fared better. Thomas Dunn himself became

a victim of bureaucratic inadequacy. After the registrar's office had been closed down he had had £200 in toto of his annual salary of £300. In June 1656 he had been owed £400; only half of that was found from militia funds. In October 1657 the Council of State was still ordering that Dunn should have £600 arrears of salary. His experiences matched exactly those of treasurers and governors of houses of correction in Devonshire; the same delays, the same need for persistent demands and the same desperate casting about for fiscal expedients.

7. Conclusions

Security and finance were the preoccupations of Interregnum legislators; no discernible pattern emerges beyond these themes. Laws controlling the maintenance of highways and establishing lay registrars of christenings, marriages and burials in each parish (another manifestation of a concern for numbers) seemed to widen the scope for participation by small freeholders. Small litigants, too, were helped by the abolition of fees which the filing of suits in Common Pleas had attracted. On the other hand, the vicious post-Restoration game laws were adumbrated in a statute of 1651 which not only allowed poachers to be convicted on oath before only one J.P. but also provided cash rewards for informers, as in the 1620s. (Informing was also stimulated by 1650 legislation aimed at uncovering concealed delinquents' estates.) The protection of property is a common, if tenuous thread here; the governments of the Interregnum were, in this respect, unexceptional.

The 'centralisation' which occurred during the 1650s was of a very specific kind. It did not develop through institutional change. The decline of the assize circuits as an agency of control by far outweighed in significance the temporary monitoring of juries and population. Here, control developed in one case as a practicable aspect of legal reform and in the other as a simple matter of State security. In neither case did change improve the performance of the tasks of government in the localities. There was no shift in the pattern of decision-making from local to central levels. If 'interference' is substituted for 'centralisation', if the major-generals are seen simply as meddlers rather than as agents of the centralising State our understanding is improved. But when historians have spoken of 'centralisation' they have meant the presence of soldiers in the counties as commissioners for assessments and for ejecting scandalous ministers. Their existence does not outweigh the drift from interference. The 'collapse' of central government interest in local government in 1660 is an illusion which the presence of the men on horseback has created among historians. Rather than centralisation in the 1650s, succeeded by a revulsion from this at the Restoration (and here interpretations of 'government' have followed the perceived fortunes of 'Puritanism'), there was probably a shift in the relationship between Whitehall and the provinces which developed steadily from the remedial legislation of 1641. Seen in this light, the major-generals appear as temporary successors to the assize judges and to the apparatus of conciliar control.

Notes

1. E.M. Leonard, The Early History of English Poor Relief (Cambridge, 1900), p.156.

2. T.B. Macaulay, The History of England from the Accession of James II (ed. T.F. Henderson, 5 Vols., 1931), Vol. i, p. 120.

3. Underdown, 'Settlement in the Counties' in G.E. Aylmer (ed.), The Interregnum (1972), p. 166.

4. H. Simon, Administrative Behaviour (New York, 1957), p. 38.

5. Ivan Roots, 'Cromwell's Ordinances' in Aylmer (ed.), The Interregnum (1972), p. 212.

6. John Norden, quoted in Eric Kerridge, Agrarian Problems in the Sixteenth Century and After (1969), p. 31.

7. W.O. Ault, 'Some Early Village Bylaws', English Historical Review, xlv (1930), p.231.

8. Brian Manning, The English People and the English Revolution (1976), p. 328.

9. Charles Blitzer, An Immortal Commonwealth: The Political Thought of James Harrington (New Haven, 1960), p. 259.

10. G.L. Haskins, Law and Authority in Early Masachusetts (New York, 1960), p. 687.

11. 'Several Draughts of Acts...' in W. Scott (ed.), Somers Tracts (13 Vols., 1809-15), Vol. vi, p. 211.

12. Reasons Against the Bill Entituled An Act for County Registers (1653), p. 20.

13. 'Several Draughts of Acts' ibid; Reasons Against the Bill, p. 7.

14. 'Sergeant Thorpe's Charge' in W. Oldys (ed.), Harleian Miscellany (8 Vols., 1744-6), Vol. ii, p. 11.

15. T. Birch (ed.), State Papers of John Thurloe (7 Vols., 1742), Vol. iv, p. 215.

16. J.S. Cockburn, A History of English Assizes 1558-1714 (Cambridge, 1972), pp. 104-5.

17. J.T. Rutt (ed.), Diary of Thomas Burton (4 Vols., 1828), Vol. ii, p. 34.

18. W.C. Abbott, The Writings and Speeches of Oliver Cromwell, (4 Vols., Cambridge, Mass., 1937-47), Vol. iv, pp. 87-88.

19. T. Birch op. cit., Vol. iv, p. 639.

20. J.S. Morrill, The Revolt of the Provinces (1974), p. 77.

21. British Library Add. Ms. 22, 546 f 123.

22. C.H. Firth, 'Thurloe and the Post Office', English Historical Review, xiii (1898), pp. 527-33.

23. C.H. Firth and R.S. Rait (eds.), Acts and Ordinances of the Interregnum (3 Vols., 1911), Vol. ii, pp. 1110-13.

24. Anthony Fletcher, A County Community in Peace and War: Sussex 1600-1660 (1975), p.304.

25. North Country Diaries, 2nd series, (Surtees Society, cxxiv, 1915), p. 52.

3. The Politics of the Army and the Quest for Settlement

DEREK MASSARELLA

1. Introduction

The politics of the 1650s are no longer seen by historians merely as an epilogue to the Civil War and prologue to the Restoration of the Stuarts in 1660. Settlement is seen as having been feasible, and for a short time under the Protectorate a substantial number of the traditional political nation appeared to be playing a more active and positive part in politics.[1] In any discussion of the attempts made to secure a settlement of the division that resulted from the Civil War and the revolution of 1648-1649 an understanding of the role of the army is crucial. The army made the revolution of 1648-1649, but it also made the Restoration of 1660, and its presence was impressed upon all the developments of the intervening years.

2. The creation of the New Model Army

The New Model Army was established by parliamentary Ordinance in January 1645. The traditional explanation of its creation was that it was part of an attempt to improve Parliament's fighting ability by establishing a national army with a unified structure directly under Parliament's control, to replace the existing mixture of armies, which had regional rather than national loyalties, and which were headed by commanders who were reluctant to act in concert.[2] Recently this view has been challenged. The New Model is said not to have marked a decisive break and that its membership, structure and financing differed little from that of previous armies, and that despite a much lower level of desertion, its cohesion owed more to luck - the need to engage the King at Naseby - than to any ideological, including religious, commitment.[3] Whether or not we subscribe to the view that the creation of the New Model marked a decisive turning point in the conduct of the war, we do know that many of its members, especially the officer corps, were volunteers who felt that they were fighting for a cause. Indeed, one of the most obvious things about the Civil War is that besides being a struggle for power it was also about issues of principle and that those who took up arms, including many members of the New Model, felt, with varying degrees of enthusiasm no doubt, that they were involved in a fight to see those issues settled. This is central to understanding why the army became a political force in 1647 and why it remained one throughout the 1650s.

I would like to thank Professor G.E. Aylmer, Professor I. Roots and Dr. Anne Lawrence for their comments on an earlier draft. The final version is, of course, my own responsibility.

3. The politicisation of the Army

The army emerged as a political force during the spring and early summer of 1647 after victory in the field had been won. By March 1647 Parliament, which was dominated by the Presbyterian peace party under the leadership of Denzil Holles and Sir Philip Stapleton, was intent on sending a part of the army to Ireland to quell the rebellion which had broken out there in 1641, maintaining some units in England and disbanding the rest. Holles, Stapleton and their supporters felt that such action would remove what they considered to be one of the greatest impediments in the way to reaching an accord with the King.[4] What they did not reckon on was the reaction within the army against these proposals.

At first the army opposed the terms for the Irish service on the grounds that they made inadequate provision for arrears, that they lacked indemnity for acts committed during the war and that they did not deal with other professional grievances. The initial impetus for this opposition came from the rank and file, but many of the officers shared the fears of the men. A sizeable number of the officers, however, were prepared to accept Parliament's terms. These became known as 'undertakers'. Under the influence of external propaganda, most of which emanated from the London Levellers, and fired by its own indignation, the majority of the army dug in its heels and refused to comply with the Parliament's orders. By June with the King under army jurisdiction – he had been seized by a troop of horse under Cornet George Joyce in an action which was not ordered by the senior command, or Grandees, but which was afterwards condoned and exploited by them – and with the undertaker officers having decided to leave, the army claimed that it was not defying Parliament merely to further its own ends, but that it was standing up for the interests of the nation as well. The claim was made succinctly on 14 June in A Declaration or representation from His Excellency Sir Thomas Fairfax, and of the army under his command. The army asserted

> that we are not a mere mercenary army, hired to
> serve any arbitary power of a state, but called
> forth and conjured by the several Declarations of
> Parliament to the defense of our own and the
> people's just rights and liberties.[5]

What had started out as essentially material grievances had become political ones; the army had entered national politics as a political force.

It quickly became confident enough to draw up its own programme for settlement – the Heads of the Proposals, the work of Commissary General Henry Ireton and Colonel John Lambert, two of the most politically gifted members of the army [6] – and to negotiate directly with the King. In late July and early August – by which time Fairfax had been made Commander-in-Chief of all land forces in England and Wales – the army became involved in the first of many struggles for power.

On 6 August it marched into London to defeat a Presbyterian attempt to seize power which had resulted in over 70 M.P.s, including the Speaker, either fleeing to the army or signing a declaration calling on the army to intervene. Its response set the character for future interventions. It showed that the army did not aim at seizing power to install itself and to impose a settlement on the nation in the manner of modern military dictatorships, although this was by no means clear to all contemporaries. It also showed that because the army could guarantee security it had acquired a considerable political strength that would enable it to become the ultimate arbiter about what sort of government was established. The point was put by Major Francis White of Fairfax's foot regiment who said before the Army Council in September that the army was

> the highest power visible in this kingdom, and if
> you see not a good Government established for the
> weale of the people, according to equity and
> reason, it will lye upon your Excellencie's and
> the Armye's account.'[7]

White's analysis, however much truth there was in it, was too unsubtle for many of his colleagues and he was expelled from the Army Council, although other criticisms of the Grandees' policy he expressed also played a part in this. He was re-admitted to the Council in December.

The Levellers had directed a lot of propaganda at the army since the spring and, despite the fact that two of their leaders, John Lilburne and Richard Overton, were in the Tower, they remained politically important. Over the summer of 1647 the Levellers grew suspicious of the continued negotiations between the Grandees and the King over the Heads of the Proposals. These negotiations were soon to break down anyway because of Charles I's intransigence and his belief that he could always give little and gain most by playing off one group against the other. The Levellers were also critical of the lack of progress in dealing with the leaders of the Presbyterian attempted coup. They feared that the Grandees would sell out to the king. To avoid this they felt that the army needed to be pushed further to the left in the hope that it could be used as a launching pad to implement their own programme for settlement, based on The Agreement of the People.

With Leveller encouragement, some of the regiments chose new agitators, or agents as they were termed, to replace the existing agitators elected by each regiment who sat as members of the Army Council. This body whose function it was to debate army policy consisted of general officers, agitators and elected officers from the regiments had been envisaged in the Solemn Engagement of the Army, drawn up in early June.[8] The Levellers alleged that the agitators had become puppets of the Grandees. Despite their success in having some of their proposals discussed at the famous debates at Putney in October, the Levellers decided to challenge the Grandees. Leveller supporters in the army, with the prompting of the London Levellers, called for a general rendezvous of the army. They hoped to use the occasion to try to swing the army behind The Agreement of the People and down a path far different from that being marked out by the Grandees. The army leadership refused to concede to a call for a general rendezvous, and instead decided that there should be three separate rendezvous which would obviously be easier to control. At the first rendezvous, at Ware on 15 November, seven regiments were designated to participate but they were joined, contrary to orders, by two more, some of whose members

defiantly wore copies of The Agreement in their hats. The regiments
were urged to stand up for The Agreement, but order and discipline were
quickly restored with Cromwell playing a leading part. The other two
rendezvous, on 17 and 18 November, passed without incident. The debacle
at Ware resolved the issue of control within the army. That was to
remain decisively with the officers and not to come from below; nor were
the officers to be dictated to from outside. The Levellers failed to
drum up enough support within the army, and almost all of the officer
corps, some of which had certainly sympathised with Leveller aims,
closed ranks and ruthlessly put down this threat to army unity.[9] A
very small number of officers openly sided with the Levellers at the
time of Ware, the most notable of whom was Colonel Thomas Rainborowe (or
Rainsborough). But in the aftermath of the mutiny, the mood was one of
reconciliation and the officers, at least, were treated leniently and
remained in the army. Ware ensured that the need to preserve army unity
remained one of the sacred principles of army policy over the next
decade. The importance of unity was expressed in an address from the
regiment of Colonel Robert Lilburne - elder brother of the Leveller John
although he did not share his younger brother's views - one of the
mutinous regiments involved in the Ware epidode, to Fairfax. The
regiment declared that

> as soldiers..., we owe all Obedience and
> Subjection to your Excellency's Authorities and
> Commands; from which we humbly conceive neither
> Birthrights, nor other Priveledges whatsoever,
> whereof we have or ought to have an equal share
> with others, can or ought in the least to
> disoblige us.[10]

4. The Army emerges as revolutionary movement

Regardless of the Levellers' attempt to whip up the army,
there had been a shift to the left anyway during the course of the year.
This was in response to a variety of factors of which the Levellers were
only one. The others were the Presbyterian-controlled Parliament, the
King, the City of London and developments within the army itself which
perceived itself and the claims it was making as threatened. It felt
that it had to respond to these threats even if this involved a
questioning and challenging of traditional authority.

After Ware there was no easing up on the army's desire to see
the achievement of a satisfactory political settlement. During the
early winter there was a period of harmony beween the Parliament, in
which the Presbyterians had suffered an eclipse of their power, and the
army. This harmony survived into the new year although by the outbreak
of the second civil war serious differences had appeared over the
question of settlement and the part of Charles I in that settlement.
Since Ware the Grandees, reflecting feeling within the army, had
hardened their attitude towards further dealings with the King. This
attitude was stiffened even more by the King's rejection in December of
the Four Bills, covering parliamentary control of the militia for twenty
years, the revocation of declarations against Parliament, the annulment
of recent royal grants and honours and royal assent to Parliament's
right to adjourn to whatever place it felt fit. The Four Bills were

designed as a sine qua non for further negotiations. Charles's confident rejection of the Bills, inspired by his decision to throw in his lot with the Scots in the desperate belief that they would re-establish him on the throne, led to the passing of the Vote of No Addresses in January 1648. It was the decision of the Commons on 28 April to suspend this vote that led to the deterioration of relations between army and Parliament. At a prayer meeting at Windsor in late April 1648 - prayer meetings often preceded important decisions or changes in policy - the officers decided that Charles Stuart 'that Man of Blood' should be brought to account

> for that Blood he had shed, and Mischief he had
> done to his utmost against the Lord's cause and
> People in these poor Nations.[11]

It was a momentous decision and marks the army's emergence as a revolutionary movement, not just a radical political one. But the decision meant that the army was in danger of manoeuvering itself into political isolation. The trial of the King was unlikely to find widespread support at Westminster, especially amongst the middle group, which had generally supported the army, let alone in the country. It also appeared that the constitutional settlement based on the Heads of the Proposals was being quietly abandoned, unless it was intended to substitute another member of the royal family as monarch, but there was no suggestion of this. The co-operation between Parliament and army manifest in December and January had evaporated. In its place there was now an impasse, an impasse that was only to be removed by the follies of the second civil war which pushed the army even further to the left and into a commited revolutionary position from which it was instrumental in bringing about not just the King's trial but his execution and also in ushering in the new Republic.

5. The Army and the Revolution of 1648-1649

The need to fight a second civil war, during which time the Presbyterians were able to stage a comeback and to secure middle group support for fresh negotiations with the King - the Treaty of Newport - had ensured that the army did not cast away the revolutionary mantle it had doned in April; indeed it tightened it. Parliament was purged, the King brought to trial and executed, the Lords abolished and England declared a Commonwealth. At the end of August 1648 Elizabeth, Countess Dowager of Lindsay, had written to Lord Montagu declaring that

> The Army is now master of the kingdom.[12]

Her observation was perhaps inaccurate when it was written - the struggle over the Treaty of Newport still lay ahead - yet it seemed a fair enough description of the state of affairs in February 1649. Or was it?

The army had certainly brought about the revolution; but it had not done so alone. It had worked closely with civilians, both parliamentary and non-parliamentary, including the Levellers whose influence and ideas had continued to be felt in the army despite Ware. But although the Levellers were an important factor in the calculations of the army leadership and their ideas were treated seriously at the time of the revolution in late 1648 and early 1649, they did not aim to outbid the officers for rank and file support at that time as they had tried to in 1647. Thus the army had not seized power unilaterally, carried out a revolution and proceeded to attempt to force a settlement on the nation. During the revolution no army dictator emerged and no individual officer masterminded the army's policy. Cromwell stayed clear of London until after Pride's Purge; Ireton, one of the most important officers shaping policy, did not display any personal ambitions during the revolutionary months; Fairfax, an excellent military commander but a weak politician, preferred to remain in the background.[13] In fact the army leadership did everything possible to try to ensure that the revolution would be limited and that hopefully it would not alienate too many people. It sought to legitimise the revolution and to further it by making these tasks the responsibility primarily of civilians and not solely of army officers. The army's own proposals for settlement, which were debated by a General Council of Officers in December 1648 and January 1649 - soldiers had not been admitted to debates since January 1648 - and eventually spelt out in the so-called officers' Agreement, were presented to Parliament for that body to consider and to implement.[14] The army did not want its actions and role to be interpreted as an attempt to set itself up in power.

But there had been a debate within the officer corps about how far the revolution should proceed and about how far the army should be prepared to advance it. It was a debate largely over means not ends and was thus very different from the one which had caused the split between undertaker and non-undertaker officers in 1647. During the discussions, which were held at Whitehall, Captain George Joyce - the man who had seized the king in 1647 and since promoted - declared that he did not doubt

> that if there was nott a spiritt of feare upon
> your Excellency [Fairfax] and the Councill [of
> Officers], that he [the Lord] would make you
> instruments to the people of the thinges that hee
> hath sett before you.

His argument was countered by Colonel Thomas Harrison in a long speech, which partly paraphrases the Declaration preceding the officers' Agreement, in which he asserted that even if, as was inevitable, the Agreement fell short of satisfying all of the godly, especially in religious questions, it would be a proof that the army did not intend to seize power for itself:

> For itt is nott a principle of man, when wee have
> brought downe such men that would have kept us
> under, to give them a libertie, butt itt is more
> of God, to putt them into such a condition
> especially as to thinges of civill concernment
> that wee neede not seeke ourselves, that wee will
> trust God and give them uppe in a common current
> againe.[15]

For Harrison this was a fundamentally different position from that which he came to hold by 1653. In 1649, like Cromwell and Ireton, he was expressing the assumption that was guiding army policy at this time. All three supported and advocated a more limited revolution, not a more thoroughgoing one which might have sought to establish new institutions designed to rubber-stamp the army's demands. The latter course is one which most modern military interventions in politics have attempted to follow in different fashions regardless of whether or not an obvious military dictator has emerged.[16] In 1649 the army was asking civilians to implement the reforms it was advocating. But civilians, especially those who as M.P.s conceived of themselves as men more traditionally responsible for politics and government, were bound to see things differently from army officers. So the seeds of conflict were sown between the army, which was keen to see reforms introduced but unwilling to seize power itself to initiate them, and a truncated Parliament, the Rump, jealous of its rights and privileges, conservative in its aspirations but viewing itself as the repository of sovereignty after the abolition of the monarchy and House of Lords.

6. The Army and the Rump

The need to secure the revolution against enemies at home and abroad in Ireland, and subsequently in Scotland, ensured that differences between army and Parliament did not get out of hand initially. From 1649 to 1651, the young Republic felt itself to be fighting for survival.

In May 1649 the Levellers once more tried to turn the rank and file against the army leadership. The Levellers had already dissociated themselves from the officers' Agreement and attacked the army leadership for duplicity. They also accused it of seeking to establish a military dictatorship. These attacks led to the arrest, in some cases re-arrest, of the Leveller leaders and their imprisonment in the Tower.[17] The mutiny in the army on their behalf and in support of Leveller aspirations was defeated at Burford. There was a final but very small Leveller mutiny at Oxford in September which was easily put down. The crushing of Leveller attempts to use the army to realise the movement's own aspirations marked the liquidation of rank and file radicalism in the army. In the 1650s the politics of the army were the politics of the officers.

The suppression of the Irish rebellion was undertaken in the summer of 1649 with the departure for Ireland of five horse regiments, including Ireton's and a new double regiment for Cromwell, and ten foot regiments. This meant that two of the army's most capable political members were out of the country on active service. Ireton remained in Ireland as Lord Deputy and acting Commander-in-Chief until his death in November 1651. His stay there and early death deprived the army of one of its most brilliant intellectual and political personalities. The conclusion that his 'exile' in Ireland was to some degree self-imposed seems inescapable. In view of the lack of evidence, the reasons for this 'exile' must remain speculative. But Ireton was not trusted by many of the Rumper M.P.s and this was made all too clear by their rejection of him - and of Harrison too - as a member of the Council of State. It is also possible that he was very unhappy with the turn of events. After all, he must have felt that he had not struggled so long and so hard, especially from 1647, and supported the extreme measures carried out during the revolution of 1648-1649 merely to see government fall into the lap of the Rump.

Cromwell himself returned triumphant from Ireland at the beginning of May 1650 and was soon leading an army of more than 16,000 officers and men in an invasion of Scotland. Cromwell was fast becoming the most powerful man in the army. Fairfax resigned his commission in June because of scruples about the Scottish invasion. He had also refused to take the Engagement - an oath of loyalty to the Commonwealth. Cromwell as the new Commander-in-Chief won two impressive victories at Dunbar on 3 September 1650 and at Worcester on the same day a year later thereby dashing the hopes of Prince Charles to gain the English throne. The army thus succeeded in establishing control of the three nations for the Parliament and it was to play a central role in guaranteeing that control for successive Interregnum governments. A strong military presence was to remain in both Ireland and Scotland until the Restoration.

The departure of the regiments for service in these two countries was to have important repercussions on the subsequent evolution of the army. It meant that for the first time since 1647 there existed important geographical divisions within the army. These divisions undermined the close contacts between the regiments which had been possible from 1647 to 1649 when most regiments were stationed in or near London. Even when they had not been within such close-call - as with the forces in Yorkshire and in the north - regular and speedy communications between the regiments had been maintained. These contacts had enabled the army to become such a decisive political force in the first place. The splitting up of the army, which was done for military reasons not political ones, first to Ireland and then to Scotland, with other forces serving abroad later on, meant that the officers in or around London came to assume the leading position in army politics. For most of the 1650s, the forces distant from London tended to follow the lead of their colleagues in the capital. The dividing of the regiments considerably weakened army unity in the long run and led to growing political divisions, so much so, that the possibility of rival factions within the army taking to the field against one another almost became a realilty. Moreover, the presence of large numbers of officers in London absent from their regiments meant that the officers ran the risk of getting out of touch with their men. This also helped weaken army unity and sapped at the army's political strength. By late 1659 rank and file morale was so low and its confidence in the officers had evaporated to such an extent that soldiers of the Lambert/Disborowe/ Fleetwood faction opposing Monck were reported to have said that

> they will not fight, but will make a ring for
> their officers to fight in.[18]

Even while the army was engaged on active service, those officers who remained in London continued to ponder ways to advance reform, and they expected the Rump to respond to their concern. Victory at Worcester meant that in the eyes of the army there could no longer be any excuse on the part of the Rump for prevarication. In August 1652 the army, after a vigorous debate among the officers in London, presented a petition to the Rump. It was a toned-down version of demands which had been made in more forceful language and presented to Cromwell. The petition made a variety of requests. Amongst other things, it called for propagation of the Gospel, abolition of tithes, law reform and a consideration of ending the present Parliament and the settling of future ones.[19] Over the course of the next few months relations between the army and the Rump deteriorated seriously as the army increasingly came to doubt the Rump's seriousness, and willingness, to introduce reform. Attempts to bridge the differences between the two failed and the eventual outcome was the dissolution of the Rump by the army on 20 April 1653.

The immediate cause of the dissolution was a fundamental disagreement between army and Parliament over the timing and probably the contents of the Bill for a new representative. The traditional view is that Cromwell and the officers dissolved the House because the Parliament ignored an informal agreement reached the previous night after discussion between themselves and some of the most influential M.P.s not to proceed with the Bill, and instead attempted to pass a Bill which included provisions for the House to recruit itself and thus perpetuate itself.[20] Recently this view has been challenged. It is alleged that the cause of the dissolution was the House's resolution to proceed with the Bill, but that this Bill was for fresh elections not for the recruitment of the House.[21] Unfortunately, the Bill itself has not survived and in its absence there can be no definite answer to the question of what its contents were. What we can be sure of, is that on the night of April 19 and 20 there was a dramatic and decisive change in the relations between the Rump and the officers and that the latter, and Cromwell in particular, felt that the reneging on the agreement of that night was yet another manifestation of the Rump's bad faith. This was the last straw. The officers' patience was exhausted, and they decided that it was time to end the Rump.

The dissolution, as obvious a display of military power as had yet been seen in politics, was spontaneous, although pressure for some sort of action against the Rump had been building up within the army. The army went ahead and dissolved the Rump without really knowing what it was going to replace it with. Thomas Harrison, by now Major General, favoured the introduction of rule by the Saints, something like a dictatorship of the godly - the Barebones Assembly which eventually succeeded the Rump was a very much watered-down experiment in this - while Lambert favoured strengthening the position of the Council of State, and thus of the executive aspect of government, to provide a counterweight to any future Parliament. Some officers, the most notable of whom was Colonel John Okey, had their doubts about the wisdom and legitimacy of the dissolution and soon made them known, but for the majority of officers, the dissolution was an end in itself. Cromwell and his brother-in-law, Colonel John Disborowe, (or Desborough), an influential officer in army politics, had been aware of the dangers inherent in a dissolution and of how vulnerable it would make the army to the change that it was aiming at dictatorship, when they had spoken to the Council of Officers in March. They asked their fellow-officers - and here one hears the voice of Cromwell - what the army would call itself if it dissolved the Rump:

a state they could not be; They answered that
they would call a new Parliament; Then sayes the
Generall, the Parliament is not the supreme
power, but that is the supreme power that calls
it.[22]

This was exactly the point. By dissolving the Rump the army was showing
to the world that it held ultimate power in the state. But such a
display was contrary to the way that the army had acted since 1647. In
1647 Major Francis White had been expelled from the Army Council for
saying that there was no visible power but that of the sword. He had of
course been correct. But this was a reality that the army had been
reluctant to accept and the officers had done everything possible to
camouflage it by co-operating with civilians. From this had followed
the limited revolution of 1648-1649 and the gradualist approach towards
reform. In April 1653 that policy appeared to be in ruins, destroyed by
the army itself, but not just by the army. The army and the Parliament
had become locked in a fearful struggle the outcome of which had to be
the demise of one or the other. In 1653 it was obvious which would go.
But the dissolution did not mean that the army was aiming at military
rule. At no stage in the 1650s did the army seek to govern by itself.
It continued to seek to establish some form of civilian government to
provide a legal and constitutional foundation to government and to
advance and legitimise reform. To that extent, the gradualist approach
to reform was salvaged from the wreckage caused by the Rump's
dissolution.

From April to July 1653 the government was in the hands of
the Captain General of the armed forces, Oliver Cromwell, who now
emerged as the leading figure in both civilian and military politics,
and an interim Council of State consisting of military and civilian
personnel – an attempt to blur the appearance of naked military rule.
The unity of the army was ensured by the distribution of a declaration
on 22 April justifying the dissolution, to which many of the regiments
sent back affirmations of support. A few officers expressed doubts
openly to Cromwell about the dissolution, and one, Captain John
Streater, had his dissensions printed, for which he was cashiered. But
there appear to have been no resignations over the dissolution. There
was much truth in Cromwell's alleged remarks when he returned to the
Council of Officers after the dissolution:

that now they must go hand in hand with him, and
justify what was done to the hazard of their
lives and Fortunes, as being advised and
concurred in it.[23]

7. The Barebone's Assembly and the Establishment of the Protectorate

Cromwell and the officers eventually rejected the sort of
leftward lunge which the Barebone's Assembly seemed to represent. The
members of the Assembly were chosen by Cromwell and the officers. The
selection process was not smooth and took over a month to complete. On 6
June summonses to individuals to sit in the Assembly were despatched on
Cromwell's name as Captain General and Commander-in-Chief. It seems as
if originally it was intended to have a measure of self-denial, whereby

any army officer nominated to the Assembly would have had to lay down
his commission.[24]   The most likely reason for this was a desire for
the new Assembly to be as civilian a body as possible, and to be
regarded as such.   But a few officers were nominated to it, and at the
beginning of the session, Cromwell, Lambert, Harrison, Disborowe and
Mathew Thomlinson were co-opted to serve in the Assembly.   With such
substantial officers as these permitted to sit in the Assembly, self-
denial could only have been a non-starter.   To enforce it would have
meant crippling the army's senior command structure and destroying its
political leadership, and the army was not bent on political hara-kiri.

It seems that Lambert was not at all happy with the creation
of the Barebone's Assembly and the rebuff of his desire for a stronger
Council of State.   He played a full part in the interim government
between the dissolution of the Rump and the establishment of Barebone's,
but when the Assembly began to sit, he withdrew from the Council of
State and by August he was reported to have retired to his residence at
Wimbledon.   However, he did not give up the political fight.   Over the
next few months he remained in or near London and was very active in
army affairs.[25]   He was popular in the army - he had been a very fair
commander during a spell in the north of England from 1647 to 1649 when
he only played an indirect part in the developments leading up to and
encompassing the revolution of 1648-1649, and his military achievements
in the Scottish campaign of 1650 were noteworthy.   Lambert's temporary
withdrawal from politics in 1653 was a shrewd move, an opportunity to
bide time, and a tactical retreat to enable a future advance.   Harrison,
on the other hand, grew disillusioned with Barebones.   He too withdrew
from the Council of State over the summer and fared badly in the
elections for the Council in November.   But his was no tactical move.
It amounted to a resignation from the political struggle.   The Saints
had a poor ally in the army leadership with Harrison.   As a leader of
the left he was not equal in stature to what Colonel Thomas Rainborowe
had been in 1647 and the adeptness at political in-fighting which he had
displayed in 1647-1649 was gone.

From about September 1653 there was a growing mutual disappointment, distrust and dissatisfaction between Cromwell and the
radical members of Barebone's.   The more it seemed to the General that
the Assembly was likely to subvert property and remove tithes without
providing an alternative source of maintenance for the preaching
ministry, the more some of the Saints correspondingly grew outspoken in
their condemnation of Cromwell.   By early December they were bitterly
denouncing him as 'the man of sin, the old Dragon'.[24]   However, they
soon over-reached themselves, and on 12 December the moderate members
moved for the Assembly's dissolution, which was carried, although the
army had to be employed to enforce the vote.   Harrison's decline - he
had little support in the army and was cashiered on 21 December - spelt
Lambert's rise.   Lambert was the draughtsman and prime mover behind The
Instrument of Government, a constitution based on an elected unicameral
Parliament, a Council and a Single Person, or Lord Protector.[27]   No
doubt he had used the time of his withdrawal to think about and draught
his proposals.   In any case he had The Instrument ready for acceptance
immediately Barebone's disappeared.

The Protectorate was established with the absolute minimum of
opposition from the army.   The process whereby Cromwell himself was
converted to it is unclear because of lack of evidence, but he was

certainly under pressure to establish some sort of written constitution which would guarantee 'fundamentals' particularly in property and religion from what moderates saw as the iconoclasm of radicals in the Barebone's Assembly.[28]   Other officers were won over by what appears to have been a vigorous lobbying campaign in favour of The Instrument by Lambert and his associates, who most likely included both officers and civilians. The establishment of the Protectorate, and its acceptance by the officers, may seem like a step backwards. After all, the army had been one of the principal advocates of a trial and execution of Charles I, and it had fought vigorously against his son and his supporters to prevent a restoration of the Stuarts. However, since 1649 nothing had been achieved by way of settlement that promised permanence. The officers were prepared, therefore, to give support to a new constitution which held out such a hope. Moreover, there was not necessarily an all-out hostility to government by a single person among the officers. The attempt to achieve settlement based on the Heads of the Proposals in 1647 had sought to limit not to destroy the power of Charles I and had been supported by most of the officers. It was finally rejected because of the uncompromising attitude of the king himself. Obviously it was going to be different if the man at the head of the government was the army's man, the General himself. Such was the extent of Cromwell's charisma and of his trust by the army that his elevation to the Protectorship did not cause the development of a serious opposition within the army. The acceptance of the title of Lord Protector was one thing, the attempt to substitute the title of King was, as it turned out, a different matter.

The Protectorate marked a clear return to the path of the limited gradualist revolution embarked upon in 1649. Government was to be largely in the hands of civilians and there were established institutions which were not weighted in the army's favour, through which it was expected reforms would be implemented. Cromwell was installed as Lord Protector on 16 December 1653, dressed in 'a plain black suit and cloak' not his army uniform, in an attempt to emphasise the non-military character of the new government – the sort of symbolic gesture which has not been forgotten by some modern military figures.[29]   The Protector did not lay down his commission. Army officers became members of the Protectorate Council and sat in the Protectorate Parliament as they had done under previous republican regimes. The army remained very much a presence in politics. Indeed one of the fundamental problems of the 1650s, and one that was never resolved, was that the immense power of the army was never institutionalised. The Protectorate, especially with Cromwell as head of government and head of the army, went some way towards a solution to the problem, but raised other questions. The arrangement was too much a consequence of Cromwell and his unique relationship with the army based on charisma, trust and shared experience in battle. Would the army always be satisfied that future Lord Protectors were as suitably qualified to incorporate the two positions? And, of course, the arrangement begged the question of exactly what the role of the army was in the state at a time when it seemed – especially after 1655 – increasingly unlikely that it would be called upon to fight another major engagement, at least in England. There were no precedents for a standing army, and was not the defence of England in times of peace better undertaken by the militia forces whose traditional function it was? The fact that officers sat on the Councils and Parliaments of the 1650s, including the 'Other House' when it was established, and were active in the civil service, for example in the Post Office or at the Admiralty, meant that the army's power was institutionalised to some extent. But these were informal, partial and, in the long term, unsatisfactory expressions of that power. For virtually the whole of the 1650s the army enjoyed immense power and very little responsibility.

8. Army opposition to the Protectorate

The only serious opposition to the Protectorate from within the army occured in late 1654 and early 1655. This involved two related affairs known as the Three Colonels' Petition and Overton's plot. The petition, addressed to Cromwell, involved Colonels John Okey, Matthew Alured and Thomas Saunders. The petition itself was drawn up by the former Leveller John Wildman and the draughting had been preceded by meetings involving a number of civilians, mostly former Levellers. The contrivers of the petition hoped to win over and build upon the support of a number of Rumper republican politicians such as John Bradshaw and Sir Arthur Haselrige. The petition claimed that the government established by The Instrument of Government was not legitimate and the petitioners urged the calling of a free and unbound Parliament as outlined in the officers' Agreement of 1649.[30]

The appearance of the petition alarmed the government because it occured at a time when the first Protectorate Parliament was in session and hotly disputing The Instrument in an attempt to revise it in the Parliament's favour. The three colonels were arrested. Okey and Alured were court-martialled and Okey was allowed to resign while Alured was cashiered. Both later supported the restored Rump when their colleagues in the Lambert/Disborowe/Fleetwood faction dissolved it in October 1659. Saunders was allowed to resign his commission. Later on he shed his republican sympathies and favoured a restoration of the Stuarts.

Copies of the petition, along with other anti-government tracts, were circulated in Scotland and Ireland. In Scotland a letter signed by various officers at Aberdeen and addressed to Major Abraham Holmes of George Monck's regiment was discovered. The letter called for a conference in Edinburgh to review the present state of affairs and to examine whether the army was able to justify before the Lord its present and past zeal in seeking reform. It soon transpired that Major General Robert Overton, a substantial figure in the army, was involved in this letter and had given his tacit approval to the idea of a conference. He was arrested and the opportunity was taken to purge him by the convenient discovery of an alleged plot to seize Monck and march into England. No convincing evidence was produced to support the charge of a plot involving Overton to overthrow the Protectorate. But Overton, who had been under suspicion for some time, remained a prisoner for five years without a trial until he was re-habilitated by the restored Rump in 1659.

The two affairs, related as they were - Overton was present at the discussions preceding the drawing up of the Three Colonels' Petition - were not symptomatic of a more widespread discontent in the army. The Three Colonels' Petition was confined to individuals, as was the discontent in the army in Scotland which had more to do with conscience rather than a conscious opposition to the Protectorate. The three colonels and their associates had little constructive to offer towards settlement. For them a free parliament was like a magic cure-all which would somehow produce a settlement. But free elections in the context of 1654 could easily have resulted in the return of Royalists and neuters, on the one hand, and uncompromising Republicans on the other, with anarchy as the outcome. The first Protectorate Parliament, which was not a 'free' Parliament, of course, should have been a warning to them.

The shallowness of the opposition to the Protectorate centering on the Three Colonels' Petition and Overton's plot was shown in an exchange between Lambert and Lieutenant General Edmund Ludlow in December 1655. Ludlow had served in Ireland as a commissioner and as Lieutenant General of the army there, but had not approved of the establishment of the Protectorate. He was finally recalled from Ireland for distributing the Three Colonels' Petition and other subversive literature. On his return to England he was brought before Cromwell and the Council. Lambert asked him by what authority he felt that he could act against the government. Ludlow replied vaguely that it was on an authority 'equal or superior to this' when he saw that 'the said authority would employ its power for the good of mankind'. Lambert, hitting the nail on the head and exposing the weakness of Ludlow's position, asked who would judge that

> for all are ready to say they do so, and we
> ourselves think we use the best of our endeavours
> to that end.

to which Ludlow limply replied, that if they did so then their crime was the less.[31] Ludlow had no convincing answer to Lambert's searching question and for the moment the rest of the officers were fully prepared to continue supporting Cromwell's government which they judged was making its best endeavours to advance reform and achieve settlement. The army still backed the gradualist approach to reform and Cromwell's policy of healing and settling, evidenced clear in an official petition from the army presented, perhaps significantly, to Cromwell and not to the Parliament in December 1654, reasserting calls for reform but pledging support for the Protector. Secretary Thurloe saw the petition as representing the army's unanimous desire to live and die with Cromwell

> both as their general in military matters, and as
> their protector in civil.[32]

There was an unshakeable belief among the members of the army that Cromwell would not use his considerable powers as Lord Protector to advance his own ends. Had he attempted to do so he would have soon found himself in trouble, for, as events would show, he could not afford to alienate his power base, the army.

9. The Major Generals

If Cromwell could count on the army not to rock the boat, the same was not true of the Parliament. By January 1655 relations between Parliament and Protector had deteriorated greatly. On 20 January the Parliament voted that control of the militia should be in the hands of the Protector and Parliament jointly – The Instrument had assigned it to the Protector – which was a step on the road to saying that it should be in the hands of the Parliament alone, something that neither Cromwell nor the army would allow. On 22 January, after five lunar months, Cromwell dissolved the Parliament, confident of the backing of the army. Within a couple of months the army was given a renewed taste of action by putting down Penruddock's rising in favour of Charles Stuart. The rising was easily supressed but it paved the way for the introduction of the Major Generals and the decimation tax, both of which were to increase sharply the army's unpopularity in such a way, and to such an extent, as had not been witnessed since the days of free quarter in 1647.

The Major Generals, with their obvious overtones of military rule and their lingering oppressive image in folk memory, were never intended to be a long term solution to the problem of settlement and they were a far cry from being a springboard for an attempt by the army and the Captain General/Lord Protector to seize complete control of government and society.

The dissolution of the first Protectorate Parliament caused by disappointment and disillusion meant that there was a lot of hard thinking about how the government of the country was to be given the substance and appearance of legality. Legislative power was left in the Protector and Parliament as laid down in The Instrument. But it seems as if, temporarily at least, the long-term question of settlement had been thrown back into the melting pot. It was out of this melting pot that the 'system' of the Major Generals emerged. The Major Generals were an expedient devised to help sort out the pressing problem of national security in the aftermath of the deep psychological blow caused by the royalist rising. The 'system' of the Major Generals evolved gradually over the summer and autumn of 1655 and the initiative for it came from the Council, not from the army itself. It was intended that the Major Generals would work in unison with the local authorities, not usurp their powers, but in this respect they were unsuccessful.

However, the government's ambitious foreign policy against the Spaniards in the West Indies – the Western Design – caused severe financial problems. After a conference of the Major Generals in London in May and June 1656, Cromwell was recommended to call a new parliament as the best way to resolve the financial crisis. The proposal was supported by a significant number of the Council. The fact that the Major Generals advocated a parliament reflects their continuing adherence to the policy of healing and settling. Cromwell, despite his initial support, which was shared by some of the Council, for extending the decimation tax, was won over to the idea of calling a parliament, no doubt impressed by the confidence the Major Generals expressed of being able to help secure one favourable to the government. In fact they failed to achieve this and a number of M.P.s whom the government felt it could not tolerate were returned. The extent of the Major Generals' failure can be grasped from a letter by Thomas Kelsey, Major General for Kent. On 26 August 1656 he wrote to Cromwell that most of the

> Cavaliers fell in with the Presbyterians against
> you and the Government, and the spirit is
> generally bitter against swordsmen, decimators,
> courtiers, etc., and most of those chosen to sit
> in the ensuing Parliament are of the same spirit.

What happened in Kent was that the traditional M.P.s in the county were returned to the Parliament. Kelsey favoured imposing a test on all M.P.s before allowing them to sit to ensure that they would not meddle with The Instrument - of which he had been one the original promoters in 1653. More ominous, and perhaps betraying his true attitude and that of many of his fellow officers to the idea of parliaments after the experiences with the Rump, the Barebones Assembly and the first Protectorate Parliament, was his declaration that he and his subordinates would stand by Cromwell 'with life and fortune' to maintain

> the interest of God's people, which is to be
> preferred before 1,000 Parliaments [33] -

a vague assertion reflecting a very simple and dangerous approach to politics. In the event a test was applied which led to the exclusion of some of M.P.s, but even so quite a number were returned and allowed to sit who, as it turned out, had very different ideas about settlement from those of the army, and who were prepared to challenge the army and its claims. More important, they were able to win over Cromwell himself to these ideas.

10. The Kingship Crisis

Cromwell had been extremely disappointed with his first parliament, and possibly with the idea of parliaments tout court, but in the end he gave in to the view that a parliament should be called. During the session he gradually changed his view and began to be impressed with the Second Protectorate Parliament's attempts to put forward proposals for settlement and by what appeared to be a genuine desire, on its part, to get on well with the Protector.[34] This does not mean that the House met in September 1656 armed with blueprints for settlement or with the necessary consensus to achieve one. As was so often the case in the 1650s, the proposals evolved in response to a crisis.

At this juncture the catalyst was James Naylor, the Quaker who entered Bristol on the back of a horse in the manner of Christ's entry into Jerusalem, for which he was brought before the House on a charge of blasphemy. Naylor's case exposed a great weakness in The Instrument. Who was to arbitrate between Parliament and Protector if the two disagreed? The proposals for settlement which emerged out of the controversy surrounding the case became known as The Humble Petition and Advice and originally included the offer of kingship. Here at last the tantalising prospect of an enduring settlement, especially as it was the work of civilians, was held before Cromwell's eyes. But to accept it in full Cromwell would have been forced to alienate large and important sections of the army; even by accepting it without the kingship clause, he was placing quite a strain on the loyalty of many officers who had followed him faithfully through all the twists and turns of the 1650s.

The offer of the crown became such a major crisis and turning point in the politics of the 1650s for many reasons. Firstly, the crisis represented a civilian/military conflict, but with both groups being internally divided as well. Secondly, The Humble Petition and Advice marked the first promising attempt at settlement to emerge from civilians. This must have caused a feeling of wounded pride among the officers and a resentment at being outflanked by civilians interfering with The Instrument, which was probably believed by many officers still to provide the best hope for settlement. Such emotions were exacerbated because they came at a time when the army itself was at a loss to come up with any alternative to The Instrument. The army had reached a stage of creative inadequacy. No doubt there was also a frightening realisation among the more perceptive officers that the civilian promoters of The Humble Petition were seeking to reduce the political power and influence of the army, and ultimately to eliminate it from politics. Thirdly, the crisis helped make the possibility of a split within the army uncomfortably real. It marked the most serious threat to unity among the officer corps since the division over the Irish service in 1647, and this threat was made all the more serious because it was taking place at the centre not on the periphery in Ireland or Scotland, for example. This emphasised just how important the officers around London were in politics. Fourthly, there was a danger of a rift between Cromwell and a sizeable number of his officers. Opposition to kingship ran quite deep amongst them. Cromwell was in no position to appeal over the heads of the officers opposing kingship to civilians and those officers supporting it, in an attempt to build a new power base. Nor could he hope to carry out 'a night of the long knives' and cashier a few of the senior officers as an example and then to follow his own course. There is a great deal of truth in Sir Charles Firth's remark that

> the officers were the representatives of Cromwell's party; the army was the constituency Cromwell represented.[35]

Obversely, there was no substantial figure in the army who felt strong enough to exploit the kingship crisis and challenge Cromwell's supremacy in the army and in politics. Unlike Napoleon's army, the English army in the 1650s was no academy for future statesmen, nor did it share the penchant of many modern military regimes for its members to play musical chairs amongst themselves with positions of power.[36] Finally, the kingship crisis reinforced the view among many of the officers that the army was the guardian of what came to be known as the Good Old Cause. The policy of healing and settling had begun to come unstuck. The army could offer nothing in its place and more than ever appeared to be an impediment in the way to achieving it.

11. The end of Oliver Cromwell's Protectorate

Cromwell rejected the offer of kingship and on 26 June 1657 he was installed for a second time as Lord Protector in a ceremony far more pompous than the previous one, and with a more obviously civilian entourage accompanying him. The political controversy did not stop with his refusal of kingship, and supporters and opponents of kingship continued to provoke each other. However, the coalition of anti-kingship officers soon began to break up and the chief loser from this was John Lambert. He used every opportunity to show his prejudice against The Humble Petition, but did not go so far as to oppose it root and branch. By early July he had isolated himself within the army, and Cromwell was able to purge him easily, and with no overt response in his favour from the army. Why was this so? The reason must lie in the fact that during the kingship crisis although there was a lot of revulsion in the army against the title of king, which finally forced Cromwell to reject it, there was also a substantial middle ground among the officers, consisting of men who opposed the title, but who were still prepared to follow Cromwell and the policy of healing and settling once that divisive issue had been laid aside. The middle ground was probably made up of officers who supported Cromwell for a variety of reasons including loyalty and a genuine belief that the fate of settlement and reform was bound up inseparably with that of the Protector. At a more mundane level, their own self-interest, especially as beneficiaries from the sales of crown lands, must have figured also. These sales needed to remain confirmed by laws and upheld by an administration of justice which, in the absence of anything else, they probably concluded was best guaranteed by sticking by Cromwell. Lambert miscalculated and under-estimated the strength of this middle ground feeling; Charles Fleetwood and John Disborowe, the other two key members of the army, probably subscribed to aspects of it, hence their desire to see the new constitution work. However, Lambert's downfall swelled the members of former officers with the most substantial figure of all.

Neither The Humble Petition, with its provision for 'the Other House' which could, if need be, act as a buffer between the Protector and the elected chamber, nor the second session of the Parliament, beginning on 20 January 1658, provided the country with settlement. Within two weeks the Parliament had been dissolved by the Protector. There was a bitter dispute in the Commons about what to style 'the Other House' while Rumper Republicans like Sir Arthur Haselrige and Thomas Scott tried to wreck the entire proceedings. There was also an attempt to stir up disaffection in the army with a petition in favour of restoring the Rump. This led to the cashiering of six officers of Cromwell's regiment, including the Major. But the rest of the army remained firmly behind him.

The future became very uncertain over the next few months in view of the Protector's deteriorating health. By the end of August when Cromwell was in his death struggle, there are indications that the army officers were at last waking up to the likelihood of his demise and were trying to prepare themselves to face up to it and to work out a response. Signs of the future division between Protectorian and anti-Protectorian officers, the latter centering on Fleetwood's residence at Wallingford House, also emerged. A number of junior officers around London also appeared as an important pressure group and remained so until the restoratin of the Rump in 1659, but they were never more than a pressure group. Cromwell's son Henry, who was serving in Ireland as Lord Deputy, portrayed the situation vividly in a letter to Thurloe at the end of June:

> Have you any settlement? Does not your peace
> depend upon his highness's life, and upon his
> peculiar skill, and faculty and personall
> interest in the army as now modelled and
> commanded? I say, beneath the immediate hand of
> God (if I know anything of the affaires in
> England) there is no other reason why wee are not
> in blood at this day.[37]

Allowing for some obvious exaggeration, especially in the last part of
the statement, it was quite a shrewd assessment of affairs at the end of
Oliver Cromwell's Protectorate.

After the death of Cromwell, the army made it quite clear
that it was going to try to win back some of the political ground it
felt that it had lost during the last eighteen months or so. Whatever
qualms the officers had had about challenging Cromwell they had few
regarding his son and successor, Richard.

In an address presented to Richard on 18 September, shortly
after his father's death, the officers wrote their own epitaph for
Oliver declaring that he had considered the army 'the choicest Saints,
his chiefest Worthies'. They urged the new Protector to ensure that the
new Privy Council – The Humble Petition and The Additional Petition and
Advise reverted to the style 'Privy Council' instead of Council of State
under the Rump, or simply Council as under The Instrument – was composed
of men 'of known Godliness, and sober Principles' and 'that they with
your Highness and your Army' should carry on the work of reform.[38]
The officers were advocating a kind of tripartite government of
Protector, Privy Council and army as the ideal solution to the problem
of settlement. It was a bold claim and went much further, and was put
in much stronger language, than anything that had been tendered to
Oliver. The address marked a renewed aggressive approach to politics by
the army; but it also marked the beginnings of serious divisions within
the army. In Ireland Henry Cromwell had a different address of loyalty
drawn up and sent it for subscription throughout the army there. In
Scotland Monck was not quite so independent as Henry, despite the fact
that the two men appear to have corresponded with each other. Fleetwood
forwarded the army's address to Monck requesting that the officers in
Scotland sign it. Monck had already set in motion his own address but
in the end dropped it in favour of the address sent from London.
However, he sent a copy of the address he had originally intended to
Thurloe, presumably to show that he was prepared to maintain his
independence. Army unity could no longer be taken for granted. It was
the collapse of army unity that was to help clear the way for the return
of the Stuarts.

12. The chaos of 1659

Politics from late 1658 to April 1660 have parallels with
those between March 1647 and January 1645. In both periods there were
great fluidity and constantly shifting alignments. But in terms of army
politics there was a difference. In the earlier period there had been
much consistency in the army's policy and, more important, there had
been firmer and more decisive leadership. In the later period these

factors were lacking. The army itself was not creating programmes for settlement as it had done for example with the Heads of the Proposals in 1647, the Remonstrance of 1648, or the officers' Agreement of 1649. There does not appear to have been the same high quality of political debate as had been manifested, for example, at Reading or Putney in 1647 or at Whitehall in 1649. Nor was there the same level of political consciousness running throughout the army as before. For the most part the rank and file were apathetic towards events by the end of the 1650s. The army still showed itself to be responsive to some of the most innovative political ideas of the day – for example, Harrington's idea of a select senate – but those ideas were no longer being developed and refined within the army's own ranks by men of the calibre of Ireton or the young Lambert, and even if they had been, there was no one with the political skills of Cromwell to try to put them into practice. The army had no clear idea of its political direction in the late 1650s. First it tried to see how far it could go with Richard Cromwell, and eventually got rid of him; then it recalled the Rump, failing to realise the extent of the ambitions and passionately-held convictions about parliamentary supremacy of men like Haselrige and Thomas Scott. It then got rid of the Rump. Then it flirted with Harringtonian notions. Gradually force came to be used as an end in itself. The army lost the ability to differentiate between the creative use of force, or 'right and might well met' (the military interventions in 1647, the revolution of 1648-1649, the dissolution of the Rump and the dissolution of Barebone's – in all of which the power of the sword had been used to help set up an alternative, and what was hoped viable, route to settlement), and its uncreative use. This became more apparent after 1657 as the army stumbled from one prop to another – Protector, Rump, Committee of Safety, Army Council – seeking some kind of crutch that could give government an appearance of legitimacy and help to establish a vision of settlement about which it had only the vaguest ideas. Insofar as the army still searched for legitimacy, there was consistency with the political role it had inherited from 1647-1649; the officers did not want to rule as a military dictatorship.

From the end of 1658 onwards, the tensions within the army, already in evidence at the time of Oliver's death, grew considerably and the army tore itself and the Good Old Cause to pieces. There was a split between Protectorian and anti-Protectorian officers in April 1659, between officers loyal to the restored Rump and those – the Lambert/ Disborowe/Fleetwood faction – opposed to its claims to be the source of military authority in October, and finally and decisively between the Lambert/Disborowe/Fleetwood faction and the army in Scotland. It was during this last episode, from October to December 1659, that the army's political role as it had existed for the previous twelve years really ceased.

The Lambert/Disborowe/Fleetwood faction, claiming to speak for the whole army, envisaged a General Council of the Army to decide the nation's future government. But in reality the faction could not claim to be representative of much. It did not represent all of its fellow officers, it did not represent the soldiery, who were to be excluded from the Council, and it most certainly did not represent any significant element of the political nation. It really only represented itself and a very small number of civilians. The contrast with 1647-1649 is obvious. If it was a fag-end of the Long Parliament which legitimised the revolution of 1648-1649, it was a fag-end of the army which attempted to further that revolution in late 1659. Faced with opposition from Monck in Scotland and from units declaring for the Rump, the faction's toehold on power gave way and the Rump was re-restored towards the end of December.

13. The Army and the Restoration

With the return of the Rump, the politics of the army were transformed. This was less the result of policies introduced by the Rump, such as a new round of purges, but more a consequence of the emergence of Monck as the most powerful man in the army and, after his arrival in London in the new year, the most powerful man in the country. Under Monck's leadership the army gradually renounced its claim to be the guardian of the Good Old Cause, and for the first time in 13 years was prepared to hand over power unconditionally to civilians who were to be given a blank cheque to decide what sort of government they wanted, even if it was obvious that this would mean the readmission of the M.P.s purged by Colonel Pride in 1648 and the return of the 'common enemy', 'the King of Scots', 'the pretended king', Charles Stuart.

This did not come about easily, nor was it predetermined, least of all by Monck when he began his march south on 1 January 1660, but arguably it was what the majority of the country wanted. Under Monck, the army acquiesced in its own political emasculation, despite uncoordinated resistance from some serving officers and purged officers. The acquiescence of the army is not surprising. By the beginning of 1660, with the exception of Monck's forces which he had purged while still in Scotland, replacing officers commissioned by the Rump over the summer with men loyal to him, and the forces in Ireland who were under the command of men sympathising with Monck after a coup against Dublin Castle in December, the army was broken and dispirited. The esprit of the officer corps was shattered, a result of the purges by the Rump over the summer of 1659, by the Lambert/Disborowe/Fleetwood faction after the October coup, and by the Rump again in January 1660. Monck compounded this by ensuring that when he came to London the regiments accompanying him were quartered there. Most of those already there were ordered to leave the capital for quarters elsewhere, but not within easy distance of each other. The object was to reduce the possibility of communications between them as in 1647. The credibility of the officers in the eyes of the nation, and in the eyes of fellow-adherents of the Good Old Cause, had also been destroyed by the events of the previous few months, and their pretensions to be the guardians of that Cause, let alone the vanguard to further it, shattered. By April 1660, after some further purging, Monck and his closest advisers decided that a clear statement from the army indicating that it would obey decisions made by the civilian authorities was needed. This took the form of a declaration from the regiments to which subscriptions were required, in some cases under threat of dismissal, to obey all commands of Monck, the Council of State and whatever the new parliament – the Convention Parliament – would determine. In the declaration the army also pledged itself not to meddle in affairs of state on the grounds that it thereby made itself a divided interest from the rest of the people.[39] In 1647 the army had claimed that it was not a divided interest, not a mercenary army, but a body of citizens in arms. This claim was the army's raison d'être for its political role in the 1650s. In 1660 the claim was being turned on its head. Instead of being employed to justify an active political role it was made to renounce such a role and to justify the army's subservience and subordination to civilian government.

The declaration was presented to Monck on 9 April, by which time it was obvious that a restoration of the Stuarts was just around the corner. On 2 May the officers declard their willingness to accept the Declaration of Breda in an Address which was forwarded to the new king. Subscriptions to the Address from those regiments not in London soon followed, and on 23 May Charles II arrived in London.

14. Conclusion

Socially and economically, many of the senior officers were members of the traditional ruling class. Most did not belong to the upper echelons of their class, but they were men of some standing in their immediate localities, although not necessarily in their counties. They are best described in Professor Everitt's words:

> They shone instead as lesser stars in the larger constellations of county gentry...[40]

The senior officers tended to have been educated formally (usually at one or other of the universities and at one of the Inns of Court) or had entered a trade. Some were younger sons. This was the sort of background of men like Henry Ireton, John Lambert, William Sydenham, Robert Lilburne, Thomas Saunders, Matthew Alured, Edward Whalley, William Goffe (son of a rector), John Jones and John Disborowe, although not all were younger sons (e.g. Ireton, Lambert, Lilburne and Sydenham). These names span a wide spectrum of political opinion and allegiance among the officers in the 1650s. They were not the sort of men who emerged as leading figures in their localities and as M.P.s soon after 1640, men like Sir William Brereton in Cheshire or John Pyne in Somerset, or even Oliver Cromwell himself. There is a definite sense in which it was only the war and their subsequent army careers which made these men politically important. One can envisage a talented man like Ireton or Lambert playing a leading role in local or even national politics in virtually any circumstances, but it is difficult to see how a Robert Lilburne, a Thomas Saunders, a Matthew Alured, a John Jones or even a John Disborowe would have reached such positions of power without the Civil War and their military careers (and in the case of Disborowe, without his family ties with Cromwell).[41] Even some of those who did not come from this background - and it must be remembered that in the army promotion usually depended upon merit - such as John Okey, in origin probably a substanital citizen of London, soon showed that they shared its style and aspirations. The argument that it was the war that helped establish politically most of the officers applies to such men as well.

The officers were also affected by what David Underdown has characterised as a conflict between

> two contradictory elements, one moderate and reformist, the other radical and revolutionary

which influenced many members of the traditional ruling class and their
attitudes and reactions to events during the Revolution.[42]
Intellectually the officers also shared with many of their contemporaries what J.G.A. Pocock has described as

> the dilemma of Cromwellian Puritanism...a dilemma
> between several modes of action.[43]

Their background and their investment in crown lands gave many senior,
and junior, officers a tendency to share in some of the accepted
assumptions about the established social and economic order. This
inhibited their revolutionary ardour. The question of law reform, which
remained one of the consistent demands of the army, provides a good
illustration of this. Would not too radical a reform of the laws have
endangered the officers' own social position and in many cases their
newly acquired wealth? The officers needed a comprehensive legal
framework legitimised by a constitution acceptable to the majority of
the political nation as much as any other landholders to secure their
social standing. They were, as a result, uneasy about casting their
fate and fortune to the winds of profound revolutionary social change.
The officers were incapable of ensuring the execution of a policy of
fundamental reform of the courts and property laws which according to
one distinguished contemporary, Sir Mathew Hale, would have made a
Restoration more difficult to achieve.[44] Nor were they capable of
giving the necessary leadership to the second component of what
Professor Conrad Russell has called the 'alliance' or

> union between the discontents of the
> Parliamentary gentry and those of their social
> inferiors

- an alliance based on Puritanism and resentment of arbitrary taxation
which had helped to cause the Civil War in the first place.[45] If the
officers had been willing to provide leadership to these 'social
inferiors' then what Russell calls the second of the two revolutions
within the English Revolution, the revolution of 1647-1649, 'the
revolution of the army', would have been more thoroughgoing.[46]

In an age which lacked political parties, the army came close
to being one. But it lacked a true political identity: whether it was
reformist/gradualist or radical/revolutionary. By and large it tended
towards the former. This crisis of identity ran deep and its
implications were more important not just for army politics but for the
English Revolution as a whole. Was the army, and in particular its
officers who shaped its policy virtually alone from late 1647, to pursue
a moderate or limited revolution or a radical one? Were the officers to
proceed cautiously along the road to reform, or risk all, especially
their gains from the sales of crown lands, by pursuing a fully-fledged
revolutionary policy which could have brought about a social revolution
the consequences of which they feared? Their inability to make up their
minds about this lies at the root of the army's politics. It was a
tragic flaw which led to the chaos of 1659 and ultimately to the downfall of the Good Old Cause.

An army made the revolution of 1648-1649; it also made the
Restoration of May 1660. But it was not really the army of 1647-1659
which brought about the latter development. It was the force under

Monck, a man keen on discipline who came to be surrounded by officers of like mind. Neither Monck nor his fellow-officers shared in this identity crisis. They had resolved it, perhaps it had never really troubled them. For them the army ought to be subservient to the civilian authorities. It was this belief which helped make the Restoration a reality, and it was this belief that the army continued to uphold after it.

Notes

1. The feasibility of settlement and the problems in the way receive a well-balanced analysis in the editor's Introduction to G.E. Aylmer (ed.), The Interregnum: The Quest for Settlement 1646-1660 (London, 1972).

2. See for example C.H. Firth, Cromwell's Army (1962 edition), pp. 31-33.

3. See J.S. Morrill, The Revolt of the Provinces (1976), pp.62-63; M. Kishlansky, 'The Case of the Army Truly Stated: the Creation of the New Model Army', Past and Present, lxxxi (1978), pp. 51-74.

4. For the background to parliamentary politics at this time and for an analysis of the terms 'Presbyterian peace party', 'Independent' and 'middle group', which still remain the categories making most sense of alignments in the Commons, see D. Underdown, Pride's Purge (Oxford, 1971). Cf. M. Kishlansky, The Rise of the New Model Army (Cambridge, 1979). Less satisfactory is J.R. MacCormack, Revolutionary Politics in the Long Parliament (Cambridge, Mass., 1973).

5. The Declaration is reprinted in part in J.P. Kenyon (ed.), The Stuart Constitution (Cambridge, 1966), p. 296.

6. The Heads of the Proposals are reprinted in S.R. Gardiner (ed.), Constitutional Documents of the Puritan Revolution (Oxford, 3rd edition, 1906), pp. 316-326.

7. British Library E 413 (17), The Copy of a Letter to his Excellency Sir Thomas Fairfax.

8. The Solemn Engagement is reprinted in J. Rushworth, Historical Collections..., (7 Vols., 1659-1701), Vol. vi, pp. 510-512.

9. Recently Dr. M. Kishlansky has attempted to show that Leveller infiltration and influence in the army was minimal, and that up to the eve of Ware material grievances were really what concerned the army (M. Kishlansky, 'The Army and the Levellers: The Roads to Putney', The Historical Journal, xxii (1979), pp. 795-823). This overlooks the existence of Leveller propaganda directed at, and circulating in, the army from at least March, the existence of contacts between the London Levellers and members of the army,

including officers, and the attempts by the Grandees to reach a
settlement with the King over the summer based on The Heads of the
Proposals. The commitment not to disband before a satisfactory
political settlement had been achieved was too deeply held to be
overturned merely by a favourable satisfaction of material
grievances. Dr. Kishlansky's view that the army was close to
disbanding in October because 'the end of [its] work was at hand'
(ibid., p.822) is unconvincing.

10. A Remonstrance sent from Colonel Lilburne's Regiment to his
Excellency Sir Thomas Fairfax, reprinted in Rushworth, op. cit.,
Vol. vii, pp. 913-914.

11. Kenyon, op. cit., pp. 318-319.

12. H[istorical] M[anuscripts] C[ommission] Duke of Buccleuch and
Queensbury at Montagu House, Vol. i, p.309.

13. Cf. some modern military interventions in politics, for example,
Spain and Franco, Chile and Pinochet (although arguably Pinochet is
more the head of a junta than an outright dictator like Franco),
S. Korea and Park Chun Hee, and again with Chun Doo Hwan. The
latter's resignation from the army does not detract from the fact
that he remains essentially an army type. He made his bid for power
while still a major general and primarily relies on the army for his
support.

14. The officers' Agreement is reprinted in D.M. Wolfe (ed.), Leveller
Manifestoes of the Puritan Revolution (repr., 1967), pp. 333-354.

15. C.H. Firth (ed.), The Clarke Papers, 4 Vols., (Camden Society, 1891-
1901), ii, pp. 175-186, passim.

16. For example S. Korea, Chile, Argentina, Uraguay and Bolivia. In
these interventions the army has been a right-wing and, in terms of
civil and political rights, a reactionary force, unlike the
intervention of the army in England during the English Revolution.
However, in both the Egyptian revolution of 1952 and the Portuguese
one of 1974 the respective armies acted as progressive forces. In
Egypt the army was progressive in the sense that under Neguib and
Nasser it overthrew the corrupt regime of Farouk and, under Nasser,
who won the power struggle within the army, becoming a virtual
dictator, it ensured that sweeping reforms, especially in agri-
culture, were introduced. In Portugal the army helped bring about
the revolution of 1974 and subsequently has guaranteed its achievements, notably the establishment of democracy. While the government
is composed of civilians, President Eanes, an army officer, in
addition to being head of state, remains Chariman of the Council of
the Revolution and Commander-in-Chief and Chairman of the General
Staff of the Armed Forces. I am very grateful to Professor Aylmer
for suggesting Egypt as a possible analogy.

17. For Leveller attacks on the army leadership see England's New Chains
Discovered and The Second Part of England's New Chains Discovered
reprinted in W. Haller and G. Davies (eds.), The Leveller Tracts,
1647-1653 (Gloucester, Mass., 1964), pp. 157-170, 172-189; The
Hunting of the Foxes..., reprinted in Wolfe, op. cit., pp. 359-383.

18. Clarke Papers, Vol. iv, p.300.

19. Journal of the House of Commons, Vol. viii, pp. 164-165.

20. S.R. Gardiner, History of the Commonwealth and Protectorate, 4 Vols., (1903), Vol. ii, pp. 251-265 provides a classic illustration of this view.

21. B. Worden, The Rump Parliament (Cambridge, 1974), pp. 337, 338, 365-366, 373, 377. Dr. Worden places considerable emphasis on an alleged letter from Henry Marten to Oliver Cromwell which denies that the Rump sought to recruit itself and that Cromwell could verify this if he cared to consult the Bill itself. But the 'letter' has more of the character and style of a draft polemic intended for publication than of a personal letter to Cromwell and therefore the reliability and authenticity of its contents are contentious. According to Dr. Worden, the Bill the Rump was discussing on 20 April would have brought about a 'free Parliament' (ibid., p. 338) but this speculation is open to doubt. Leaving aside the question of what the Rumpers must have realised would be the most likely response of the army to such a Bill, many M.P.s must have been aware of what a free parliament would probably have meant in 1653 - a reaction against the revolution of 1648-1649, and possible even attempts to secure the return of the Stuarts which, if successful, would have meant that many Rumpers could have found themselves being held responsible for the trial and execution of Charles I. For all its alleged conservatism, there were even more conservative elements outside the Rump and many Rumpers must have been conscious of the dangers a free parliament might hold for them, if not on ideological grounds, then at least in terms of their own safety.

22. C.H. Firth, 'Cromwell and the Expulsion of the Long Parliament in 1653, English Historical Review, viii (1893), p. 528.

23. J. Heath, Flagellum (1679), p. 128.

24. Clarke Papers, Vol. iii, pp. 4, 7.

25. C[alendar of] S[tate] P[apers] D[omestic] 1652-53, pp. 332, 341, 342, 377, 387, 395, 410, 421, 451; O. Ogle, W.H. Bliss and W.D. Macray (eds.), Calendar of the Clarendon State Papers, 3 Vols., (Oxford, 1869-1876) Vol. ii, pp. 205-206, 246; Calendar of State Papers...Venice 1653-54, pp. 124-125; C.H. Firth (ed.), Scotland and the Commonwealth, (Scottish History Society, xviii), 1895, p.238; T. Birch (ed.), State Papers of John Thurloe, 7 Vols., (1762) Vol. i, p. 393. For a different view of Lambert's movements during these months see A. Woolrych, 'Oliver Cromwell and the Rule of the Saints', in R.H. Parry (ed.), The English Civil War and After (1970), p. 71.

26. Thurloe, op. cit., i, p. 621.

27. The Instrument of Government is reprinted in Gardiner, Constitutional Documents, pp. 405-417.

28. Ibid., pp. 591-592.

29. Thurloe, op. cit., i, p. 632.

30. The petition is calendared in the C.S.P.D. 1653-54 pp. 302-304 under 1653 instead of 1654.

31. C.H. Firth (ed.), Memoirs of Edmund Ludlow, 2 Vols., (Oxford, 1894) Vol. i, pp. 434-436.

32. R. Vaughan, The Protectorate of Oliver Cromwell, 2 Vols., (1879) Vol. i, pp. 87-88.

33. C.S.P.D. 1656-1657, pp. 87-88; A. Everitt, The Community of Kent and the Great Rebellion 1640-60 (Leicester, 1966), pp.294-295. Cf. H.M.C. Portland, Vol. iii, p. 208.

34. Cf. Professor Underdown's argument that by 1657 many of the older families in the counties were beginning to accept the Protectorate and to return to active politics, and thus it made a more positive contribution to the problem of settlement (D. Underdown, 'Settlement in the Counties 1653-1658', in Aylmer (ed.), The Interregnum, p. 177).

35. C.H. Firth, The Last Years of the Protectorate, 2 Vols., (1909) Vol. i, p. 138. For a different view see H.R. Trevor-Roper, 'Oliver Cromwell and his Parliaments', in Religion, the Reformation and Social Change (2nd edition, 1972), pp. 345-391, esp. p. 384.

36. For example cf. Argentina and its recent change of President from Videla to Viola.

37. Thurloe, op. cit., p. 218.

38. The address is reprinted in The Old Parliamentary or Constitutional History of England (24 Vols., 2nd edition, 1761-1763), Vol. xxi, pp. 233-236.

39. The declaration is printed in Sir Richard Baker, A Chronicle of the Kings and Queens of England (continued by Edward Phillips) (1684), p.697.

40. Everitt, op. cit., p. 34. Cf. G.E. Aylmer, The State's Servants (1973), p. 328.

41. It should of course be remembered that Fleetwood, Richard Ingoldsby and John Reynolds came from county gentry backgrounds, but they were also younger sons. Fleetwood and Ingoldsby were also related to Cromwell.

42. Underdown, Pride's Purge, pp. 8, 353.

43. J.G.A. Pocock, The Machiavellian Moment (Princeton, N.J., 1975), p. 338.

44. M. Hale, Some Considerations Touching the Alteration of Laws, quoted in D. Veall, The Popular Movement for Law Reform 1640-1660 (Oxford, 1970), pp. 228-229.

45. C. Russell (ed.), <u>The Origins of the English Civil War</u> (1973), p. 27.

46. <u>Ibid</u>., p. 3. Professor Russell's notion of the two revolutions echoes but is not the same as Dr. Hill's concept of the two revolutions in the mid-seventeenth century (C. Hill, <u>The World Turned Upside Down</u> (1973), p. 12). For the reasons given above, the army was not able to ensure the success of Dr. Hill's second revolution (the establishment of communal property, more democracy in politics and law etc.).

BIBLIOGRAPHICAL NOTES

Introduction : the Interregnum

This could become an endless enterprise. The items cited below will lead the student to further reading of both primary and secondary material which should both satisfy and stimulate his curiosity.

The standard bibliography is G. Davies (ed.), Bibliography of British History: Stuart Period 1603-1714, revised F.M. Keeler (Oxford, 1970). It may be supplemented by W.C. Abbott (ed.), Bibliography of Oliver Cromwell (Cambridge, Mass., 1929). For more recent work see J.S. Morrill's Seventeenth Century Britain 1603-1714 (Folkestone, 1980), one of a series of 'critical' bibliographies. The fullest narrative remains S.R. Gardiner's monumental The History of the Great Civil War (4 vols., 1893), and The History of the Commonwealth and Protectorate (4 vols., 1903) – unlikely even after nearly a century to be replaced. It was completed by C.H. Firth, The Last Years of the Protectorate (2 vols., 1910) *and G. Davies, The Restoration of Charles II (Oxford, 1955). Briefer are C.V. Wedgwood, The King's Peace 1637-1641 (1955) and The King's War 1641-1647 (1958); R. Ashton, The English Civil War 1603-1649 (1978) with the subtitle 'conservation and revolution' – although in a series on 'great revolutions', this stresses the former quality of the period; and, underlining the significance of the 1650s, I. Roots, The Great Rebellion 1642-60 (4th edn., 1978). Two contrasting text-books, the one chiefly narrative, the other analytical, but each putting the Interregnum into the perspective of the whole seventeenth century, are B. Coward, The Stuart Age (1980) and C. Hill, The Century of Revolution (revised edn., 1980).

Several collections of articles, mostly well-documented and with bibliographies, bring out the diversity of interests and approaches of specialists in the period: C. Russell (ed.), The Origins of the English Civil War (1973); G.E. Aylmer (ed.), The Interregnum: the Quest for Settlement 1646-1660 (1972); R.H. Parry (ed.), The English Civil War and After 1642-58 (1970); B.S. Manning (ed.), Politics, Religion and the English Civil War (1972); D. Pennington and K. Thomas (eds.), Puritans and Revolutionaries: Essays in Seventeenth-Century English History (Oxford, 1978). Christopher Hill, the recipient of the Pennington and Thomas festschrift, has collected his many articles in various volumes, e.g. Puritanism and Revolution (1958) and Change and Continuity in the Seventeenth Century (1974). R.C. Richardson has briefly surveyed inter-pretations from the Restoration to the 1970s in The Debate on the English Revolution (1976).

Union and Disunion in the British Isles 1637-1660

The works mentioned here are additional to those cited in the
Notes. There is no general history of the British Isles in this period.
Works on England tend to see the events through distorting English
spectacles, on Scotland though Scottish and so on. There are a few
surveys of Anglo-Scottish relations among which D. Nobbs's short England
and Scotland 1560-1707 (1952) still has something worthwhile to say.Most
recent is W. Ferguson, Scotland's Relations with England: a Survey to
1707 (Edinburgh, 1977). There are many works about the Union of 1707
but little on that of the crowns or on the Cromwellian union of the
1650s. Details of some of these writings can be found in Ferguson and
in other works cited in the Notes to this article. Much of the material
is of a polemical nature, like Ferguson's own book, intelligent though
it is. The present author hopes that his article will go some way to
dispelling an impression given by The Great Rebellion that his sub-
conscious anti-Scottish prejudices are 'invincible' (Ferguson, op. cit.,
p. 306). Polemic also features often enough in works on Anglo-Irish
history and (far fewer available) on Irish-Scottish and (fewer still)
Anglo-Welsh and Irish-Welsh history. There is almost nothing on Scotto-
Welsh relations. The author is shamefully aware of the neglect of Wales
in this article but apart from the polished pioneering work of A.H.
Dodd, mostly, but not entirely, collected in Studies in Stuart Wales
(Cardiff, 1952), a few articles in various local journals and histories
(e.g. by A.M. Johnson in G. Williams (ed.), Glamorgan County History,
Vol. iv, 1536-1770 (Cardiff, 1974) and again in the Hill festschrift),
there is little really relevant. The Welsh History Review has been less
productive of pertinent work than have The Scottish Historical Journal
and Irish Historical Studies.

To list further items on England would only encourage the
English centricity which this article would wish to dissipate. Besides
works on the other kingdoms mentioned in the Notes the following are
worth attention: T.W. Moody et al., (eds.), A New History of Ireland,
vol. iii, 1534-1691 (Oxford, 1976) with a full bibliography; almost
anything by J.C. Beckett, notably The Making of Modern Ireland (1966),
where the term 'the war of the three kingdoms' is employed,
Confrontations (1972) with a chapter on 'Irish-Scottish Relations in the
Seventeenth Century' and The Anglo-Irish Tradition (1976) with studies
of 'England's oldest colony' and 'the foundation of the Protestant
ascendancy'.

For Scotland attention is drawn to S.G.E. Lythe's The Economy
of Scotland in the European Setting 1550-1625 (Edinburgh, 1976) which,
though breaking off before our period, has much to suggest for it.
L. Kaplan's brief Politics and Religion during the English Revolution
(1976) is in fact a study of negotiations between Parliament and
Covenanters in the early 1640s. There is a valuable article on 'The
Cromwellian Union: The Case of Aberdeen and Glasgow 1652-60' by T.M.
Devine in J. Butt and J.T. Ward (eds.), Scottish Themes: Essays in
Honour of S.G.E. Lythe (Edinburgh, 1976). Much may be expected of the
forthcoming volume (in the 'New History of Scotland' series) by
R. Mitchison The Union of the Crowns and Union of the Kingdoms (1981).
Original sources are too complex and numerous to set out here. They may
be traced in the bibliographies and references in items cited above.

Local Government Reform in England and Wales During the Interregnum : A Survey

For ideas on local government, Mary Cotterell, 'Interregnum Law Reform: the Hale Commission of 1652', English Historical Review, lxxxiii (1968), pp. 689–704 and Donald Veall, The Popular Movement for Law Reform 1640–1660 (Oxford, 1970) are useful surveys but through W. Haller and G. Davies (eds.), The Leveller Tracts 1647–1653 (Gloucester, Mass., 1964) the reader may trace the development of Leveller views for himself. See also G. Winstanley, The Law of Freedom, ed. Christopher Hill (Harmondsworth, 1973) and Hobbes's Leviathan.

On the mechanics of local government Sidney and Beatrice Webb, English Local Government from the Revolution to the Municipal Corporations Act: The Parish and the County (1906) should be read with the more recent treatments by, for example, L.M. Hill in C. Russell (ed.), The Origins of the English Civil War (1973) and G.C.F. Forster, 'County Government in Yorkshire during the Interregnum', Northern History, xii (1976), pp. 84–104.

Full-length county studies are legion. Of particular interest are A.M. Everitt, The Community of Kent and the Great Rebellion (Leicester, 1966); D. Underdown, Somerset in the Civil War and Interregnum (Newton Abbot, 1973); J.S. Morrill, Cheshire 1630–1660: County Government and Society during the English Revolution (Oxford, 1974); and B.G. Blackwood, The Lancashire Gentry and the Great Rebellion (Manchester, 1978) and A. Fletcher, A County Community in Peace and War: Sussex 1600–1660 (1975). Mary Coate, Cornwall in the Great Civil War and Interregnum 1642–1660 (Oxford, 1933) is a classic. For a Welsh shire see A.M. Johnson, 'Politics and Religion in Glamorgan during the Interregnum' in G. Williams (ed.), Glamorgan County History, iv (Cardiff, 1974). Apart from these and other published works cited in the text, Robin Silcock, 'County Government in Worestershire 1603–1660' (London PhD 1974), Anne Hughes, 'Politics, War and Society in Warwickshire 1620–1660' (Liverpool PhD 1980) and S.K. Roberts, 'Participation and Performance in Devon Local Administration 1649–1670' (Exeter PhD 1980) are among the most recent doctoral theses. Dr Hughes and Clive Holmes's, 'The County Community in Stuart Historiography', Journal of British Studies, xix (1980), pp. 54–73 together offer a substantial modification of what once seemed a consensus on the concept of the 'County Community'. A highly original and fruitful approach is that of Keith Wrightson and David Levine in Poverty and Piety in an English Village: Terling 1500–1700 (1979). G.E. Aylmer and J.S. Morrill (eds.), The Civil War and Interregnum (1979) is a useful survey of 'sources for local historians'.

Studies of specific local institutions are more difficult to find. S. Morrill, The Cheshire Grand Jury 1625–59 (Leicester, 1976) and Keith Wrightson, 'Two Concepts of Order: Justices, Constables and Jurymen in Seventeenth-century England' in J. Brewer, J. Styles, An Ungovernable People? (1980) are social interpretations of the local systems of justice. The fortunes of constables may be traced in editions of quarter sessions records, such as that by D.H. Allen for Essex (1974). J.C. Hemmeon, The History of the British Post Office

(Cambridge, Mass., 1912) is the standard work. See also H. Robinson, The British Post Office in History (Princeton, N.J., 1948).

Government policy may be traced in C.H. Firth and R.S. Rait (eds.), Acts and Ordinances of the Interregnum, (3 vols., 1911) and in the Calendars of State Papers Domestic. On fiscal matters Maurice Ashley, Financial and Commercial Policy (Oxford, 1934) is still the only work available.

A recent contribution to the debate on poor relief is the essay on the London workhouse by Valerie Pearl in D.H. Pennington and K. Thomas (eds.), Puritans and Revolutionaries: Essays in Seventeenth Century History Presented to Christopher Hill (Oxford, 1978).

British Library Add. Ms. 19516, Add. Mss. 34011-17 are the Ms letter-book and lists of the registered citizens kept by Thomas Dunn and the major-generals. The experience of one county during the period of registration may be assessed in A.R. Bax, 'Suspected Persons in Surrey during the Commonwealth', Surrey Archaeological Collections, xv (1899), pp. 164-89. The Thurloe State Papers, ed. T. Birch, (7 vols., 1742) are, of course, indispensable. G.E. Aylmer, The State's Servants (1973) is primarily a study of bureaucracy but is valuable for its insights into local administration.

Finally, the flavour of the 1650s is conveyed in the diaries and notebooks of county gentlemen who lived through them. See the note-book of Captain John Pickering in Thoresby Society Publications, Miscellanea iv and v (1904, 1909), the papers of Sir William Boteler in Bedfordshire Record Society, xviii (1936), the autobiography of Sir John Gibson, Surtees Society, cxxiv (1915), the edicts of Martin Pyke, J.P. and Thomas Delavall, J.P. in Sussex Archaeological Collections, xx, Surtees Society, lxxxiv, and the remarkable Diary of Ralph Josselin edited by Alan Macfarlane (1976).

The Politics of the Army and the Quest for Settlement

For an understanding of the structure and organisation of the army C.H. Firth's, Cromwell's Army (1962 edition), remains unchallenged. Despite the shortcomings of the chapter on politics, it is the best introduction to the army. The histories of the various regiments are traced in C.H. Firth and G. Davies, The Regimental History of Cromwell's Army, 2 vols. (Oxford, 1940), an essential work of reference.

Accessible source material for army politics can be found in W.C. Abbott (ed.), Writings and Speeches of Oliver Cromwell, 4 vols. (Cambridge, Mass., 1937-1947); T. Birch (ed.), State Papers of John Thurloe, 7 vols., (1762); C.H. Firth (ed.), The Clarke Papers, 4 vols. (Camden Society, 1891-1901); J. Rushworth, Historical Collections..., 7 vols. (1659-1701). This can be supplemented by material in the relevant volumes of the Journal of the House of Commons, Journal of the House of Lords and Calendar of State Papers Domestic.

Sources relating to the army and covering specific aspects of
the period can be found in G.R. Bell (ed.), Memorials of the Civil War:
comprising the Correspondence of the Fairfax Family, 2 vols. (1849);
G.E. Aylmer (ed.), The Levellers and the English Revolution (1975);
W. Haller and G. Davies (eds.), The Leveller Tracts 1647-1653
(Gloucester, Mass., 1964); A.L. Morton (ed.), Freedom in Arms (1978) on
the Levellers; D.M. Wolfe (ed.), Leveller Manifestoes of the Puritan
Revolution (repr. New York, 1967); B. Taft, 'Voting Lists of the Council
of Officers, December 1648', Bulletin of the Institute of Historical
Research, lii, 1979; A.S.P. Woodhouse, Puritanism and Liberty (3rd
edition 1974), covers 1647-1649; J.T. Rutt (ed.), Diary of Thomas Burton
4 vols. (1828) for the Protectorate Parliaments, including Richard
Cromwell's; C.H. Firth, 'Cromwell and the Crown', English Historical
Review, xvii, xviii, (1902, 1903) for the kingship crisis; D. Underdown,
'Cromwell and the Officers, February 1658', English Historical Review,
lxxxiii (1968); F.P.G. Guizot, History of Richard Cromwell, 2 vols.
(1856), esp. the Appendices.

Discussions of the army will be found in all the major
narratives of the period from S.R. Gardiner onwards and in monographs
and articles dealing with related subjects (see G. Davies and
M.F. Keller (eds.), Bibliography of British History. Stuart Period,
1603-1714 (Oxford, 1970); and J.S. Morrill, Seventeenth-Century Britain
1603-1714 (Folkestone, 1980).

Modern historians are beginning to look again closely at the
army. M. Kishlansky, The Rise of the New Model Army (Cambridge, 1980)
deals controversially with, amongst other things, the creation of the
New Model and its politicisation in 1647. Covering much the same ground
but easier to follow and with a better presented argument are two
articles by Kishlansky, 'The Case of the Army Truly Stated: the Creation
of the New Model Army', Past and Present, lxxxi (1978), and 'The Army
and the Levellers: The Roads to Putney', Historical Journal, xxii 1979.
For different interpretations of some of the events surrounding the
creation of the New Model see G. Holmes, The Eastern Association
(Cambridge, 1975) and A.N.B. Cotton, 'Cromwell and the Self Denying
Ordinance', History, lxi (1977).

The politicisation of the army and the influence of the
Levellers receive a different perspective from Kishlansky in
J. Gentles, 'Arrears of Pay and Ideology in the Army Revolt of 1647', in
B. Bond and I. Roy (eds.), War and Society: a Yearbook of Military
History (1975). Unfortunately it contains some serious factual errors.
See also J.S. Morrill, 'Mutiny and Discontent in English Provincial
Armies', Past and Present, lvi, (1972); J.S. Morrill 'The Army Revolt of
1647', in A.C. Duke and C.A. Tamse (eds.), Britain and the Netherlands,
VI: War and Society (The Hague, 1977); D. Underdown, 'Honest Radicals in
the Counties, 1642-1649' in D. Pennington and K. Thomas (eds.), Puritans
and Revolutionaries (Oxford, 1978).

Published work dealing specifically with army politics in the
1650s is very thin but two modern works dealing with politics with
considerable bearing on army politics, D. Underdown, Pride's Purge
(Oxford, 1971), mostly about 1647-1649 but with perceptive comments on

the 1650s, and B. Worden, The Rump Parliament (Cambridge, 1974), must be mentioned.   B.   Taft,'The Humble Petition of Several Colonels of the Army: Causes, Character and Results of Military Opposition to Cromwell's Protectorate', Huntingdon Library Quarterly, xlii (1978), discusses the Three Colonels' Petition but argues unconvincingly that it was symptomatic of widespread discontent in the army.   D.W. Rannie, 'Cromwell's Major Generals', English Historical Review, x (1895) and I. Roots, 'Swordsmen and Decimators - Cromwell's Major Generals', in R.H. Parry (ed.), The English Civil War and After (1970) consider the Major Generals.

For the units outside England J.D. St. John Seymour, The Puritans in Ireland 1647-1661 (repr. Oxford, 1961) and T.C. Barnard, Cromwellian Ireland (Oxford, 1975) make some reference to the army in Ireland but seriously misrepresent the aims and influence of the Baptist officers. Aspects of army politics in Scotland are treated in F.D. Dow, Cromwellian Scotland, 1651-1660 (Edinburgh, 1979) and in Flanders in C.H. Firth, 'Royalist and Cromwellian Armies in Flanders 1657-1662', Transactions of the Royal Historical Society, N.S. xvii (1903).

Biographies, of uneven quality, of some of the most important officers include M. Ashley, Cromwell's Generals (1954); M. Ashley, General Monck (1977); J. Berry and S.G. Lee, A Cromwellian Major General: The Career of Colonel John Berry (Oxford, 1938); W.H. Dawson, Cromwell's Understudy: The Life and Times of General John Lambert (1938); G.E. Lucas Phillips, Cromwell's Captains (1938); R.W. Ramsey, Henry Ireton (1949); C.H. Simpkinson, Major General Harrison (1905); H.G. Tibbutt, 'Colonel John Okey', Bedfordshire Historical Society, xxxv (1934). Biographies of Oliver Cromwell are legion.   But attention may be drawn to G.E. Aylmer, 'Was Oliver Cromwell a Member of the Army in 1646-7 or not?', History, lvi (1971); and C. Hoover, 'Cromwell's Status and Pay in 1646-47', Historical Journal, xxiii (1980).

Dr Derek Massarella was a student in the Department of History from 1969-72. He was awarded a Ph.D. by the University of York in 1978 for a dissertation on the politics of the Cromwellian Army. He is currently a lecturer at the Chuo University in Tokyo, and is undertaking research into Anglo-Japanese relations in the seventeenth century.

Dr Stephen Roberts was awarded a Ph.D. by the University of Exeter in 1979 and from 1979-80 was a tutor in the Department of History and Archaeology. He is currently a research assistant for the National Coal Board's History of the British Mining Industry and is a tutor for the Open University. He has published articles in Southern History and The Bulletin of the Institute of Historical Research.

Professor Ivan Roots is Professor of History and Head of the Department of History and Archaeology at Exeter. His publications include The Great Rebellion 1642-60 (4th edn. 1978), Cromwell: A Profile (1972) and 'Die Englische Revolution' in the Propylaen-Weltgeschichte. He is President of the Cromwell Association.

The cover illustration is based on an engraving by George Vertue of the Protectorate Great Seal for Scotland struck by Thomas Simon, Chief Engraver of the Mint to Charles I, the Commonwealth, the Protectorate and to Charles II.